P9-CRW-496

PROJECT MANAGEMENT PROFESSIONALS ARE

Coloring Outside the Lines™

FROM THE CRAYON OF:

Jeff Tobe and Ted Kallman

Drawings by Jordan Tobe, age 12

COTL Press

PITTSBURGH, PENNSYLVANIA

Special Edition © 2015-2016 Jeff Tobe and Ted Kallman. Printed and bound in the United States of America. All rights reserved. No part of this book may be reproduced or transmitted in any form or by any means, electronic or mechanical, including photocopying, recording, or by an information storage and retrieval system—except by a reviewer who may quote brief passages in a review to be printed in a magazine, newspaper, or on the Web—without permission in writing from the publisher. For information please contact Coloring Outside the Lines, 5311 Friendship Avenue, Pittsburgh PA.

Although the author and publisher have made every effort to ensure the accuracy and completeness of information contained in this book, we assume no responsibility for errors, inaccuracies, omissions or any inconsistency herein. Any slights of people, places or organizations are unintentional.

SPECIAL EDITION printing 2015

ISBN   **978-1515256878**

LCCN   **1515256871**

ATTENTION CORPORATIONS, UNIVERSITIES, COLLEGES AND PROFESSIONAL ORGANIZATIONS: Quantity discounts are available on bulk purchases of this book and the book can be completely customized for your organization to fit specific needs. Contact us at 1-412-759-5319 or at Coloring Outside the Lines, 5311 Friendship Avenue, Pittsburgh, PA 15224

This book is dedicated to those unsung heroes
of the project management world....

contents

If you Can't Win the Game...   1
On Competition and Changing the Way You Look at Business

Lessons from the Pump   7
Do people go Out of Their Way to do Business with You?

The Rock   11
As Long as Your Goal Doesn't Change and They Use the Tools
You Give Them—

The Opportunity   17
Reframing Your Professional Problems

The Harvey Principle   21
How to See Invisible Opportunities

If It Is Broke, Don't Fix It...Yet   47
Stop Trying to Solve Your Clients' Challenges Too Quickly

Step Into My Office   53
Shattering the Stereotype of Doing Business With You

The Most Powerful Words...   61
How to Get "Buy In" Once You Are Creative

To Err is Right...or at Least Necessary   73
Taking the Fear Out of Being Successful

86 the Onions   81
We Need to Stop Being So Critical of our Own Ideas

House On Wheels   87
Get Outside Your Comfort Zone to Find Answers

A Modern Fairy Tale   91
See the World Through Your Clients' Eyes and Change Your Perspective

What This Means To You Is...   97
The Real Scoop on Benefits Versus Features in Your Business

Why Different Can Be Good   103
Re-Creating the Category in Which You Currently Compete

The Sunshine State   111
Understanding the Four Market Sectors to Whom We Must Appeal

Are Your Bagels Hot?   117
How to Appeal to All of the Senses of Your Customers

Does Customer Service Have Anything to do with Marketing?   123
Word of Mouth tells Others About YOU!

Experience Customer Service   129
It's Gone Beyond Customer Service

What Comes After the 'But'?   133
Becoming More Customer-Centric

Bye! Bye! So Long! Farewell!   139
Who are your BEST customers?

What the Group, "One Direction" Can Teach Us About Customer Experience   145
How EXPERIENCE shapes our strategy

My Pizza Joint is YOUR competition!   155
Knowing Your Market Better than Anyone Else

How Well Do You Know Your Customer?   161
Do You Know Your Customers' Buying Styles?

Salesperson Appreciation Day 171
How Creativity and Sales Go Hand-in-Hand

Frequent Flier Pointers 177
Four Lessons We Need to Know About Our Clients

Motivation Is Us! 185
Five Truths That Prevent You From Motivating Others

It's Kind of Hard to Explain 193
People Do Business With People Who Seem to Love What
They Do for a Living

Listen to Your World... 199
Effective Listening Techniques to Make You a Better
Management Professional

That is The Question 207
Digging Deeper to Understand your Clients' True Needs

COLORING THE POEM... 217

From Ted Kallman FCP, FCT, PMP, PMI-ACP, CSM, CSPO, CSP

I met Jeff Tobe in Pittsburgh PA during the summer of 2015 when he was the keynote speaker for the final day of PMI's Region 4 Meeting. He was without question the best presenter of the weekend and I thoroughly enjoyed his session.

I did not want to stand in the long line to purchase his book "Coloring Outside The Lines" (COTL) so on the following Tuesday I called the number on his website to see about ordering one. Jeff answered the phone and we had a wonderful chat for over an hour about his work, my work and PMI. During that call I predicted a number of things that I felt would happen as a result of his very compelling presentation in Pittsburgh. One week later he called me back because every one of my predictions came true (Including his being asked to present a Keynote address at the PMI® Leadership Institute Meeting 2015-North America).

Since I have had some experience as a writer in PM circles, Jeff graciously asked if I would consider partnering with him to add project management specific stories and examples to a revised version of COTL targeted to project managers. Of course I said yes and here we are.

Historically, project managers are not known as a creative breed. PMs are the people you call when something needs to get done, or when current chaos needs to be mud-wrestled into a cogent result. They map the reality of what has been asked for, create and offer up a plan that delivers it on scope, on time and on budget. Who needs creative?

Right?

Wrong.

The best PMs that I know are some of the most creative and innovative people in the universe. They have focused their creativity within the field of project management but they are massively creative by and standard of measurement. This book is for them. To affirm some of the things they already know and do but also to give them some new tips and tricks for their creativity tool box.

This book is also for the detail-oriented project manager who does not believe that creativity has any place in a well-run project. The PM who approaches their work with the attitude of Joe Friday from the old TV show, Dragnet holding up their hand and saying, "Just the facts ma'am, just the facts." In today's fast moving rapidly changing business and social environments we need to be more creative and innovative in how we do what we do or the world will pass us by. For those people who are not sure this applies to them we say 'welcome aboard' and ask you to trust that this book will be a thought-sparking journey into a more creative and satisfying life as project manager.

By the way, all of the buzz about Agile Project Management that has risen in the past few years has occurred in part because of the creativity and innovation these methods have loosed. Clear short horizon goals are handed off to teams that figure out how they will deliver the successful completion of those goals. Agile teams are constantly creating and innovating new solutions and improvements and as a result productivity and satisfaction improve. Captain David Marquet in his book *Turn the Ship Around* explains his approach (which is highly 'agile' without the visible aspects) as, "Provide your people with the objective and let them figure out the method." In other words, know where you are headed but let your people creatively decide the path for their portion of the journey. Push authority and decision-making to the lowest responsible level.

We also know that as you, the project manager, increase your creativity you will increase your job satisfaction and the satisfaction of your team.

Daniel Pink in his book "Drive: The Surprising Truth About What Motivates Us" talks about the difference between these two approaches. He calls the first approach Heuristic and the second one Algorithmic. Algorithmic is any work that can be planned and executed without thought, if it is not physical in nature someone somewhere is writing a computer program to replace the worker. Heuristic, or knowledge work, requires ongoing thought and adaptation. McKinsey & Company estimates that only thirty percent of job growth in the USA comes from algorithmic work. Seventy percent comes from Heuristic. Also, Heuristic work has job satisfaction in the eighty plus percentage range.

Pink presents the different creative outcomes of these approaches this way; (Amabile is a Harvard researcher he is quoting) "Amabile calls it the intrinsic motivation principle of creativity, which holds in part: "Intrinsic motivation is conducive to creativity; controlling extrinsic motivation is detrimental to creativity." In other words, the 'letter of the law' facts-driven project manager will be less creative than the intrinsically-driven and self-motivated Heuristic project manager. And research shows that intrinsically motivated people are not only more creative but also have higher job satisfaction.

It is good to be creative.

What blocks this from happening? Disengagement. Gallop had a study this year that showed over 50% of the workforce in America feels disengaged in their work. Brene Brown in her great book, *Daring Greatly*, on shame and its effects on people and organizations says, "No Corporation or school can thrive in the absence of creativity, innovation, and learning, and the greatest threat to all three of these is disengagement." So, although we recognize the need for creativity and innovation to confront the challenges of today's knowledge economy we seem to be fostering practices and cultures that prevent it from happening.

We need to change. If you are leading a project you can begin now to foster a culture of trust, vulnerability and openness regardless of the challenges you face in the overall culture you are operating within. From this platform your team can begin to freely express creative ideas and solutions as a part of the ethos and you will find performance, engagement and satisfaction will improve. Strong results will naturally follow.

Earlier in her book, Brene mentions that you cannot give what you do not have. In other words this culture starts with you. Find ways to become more vulnerable, open and trusting. Expand your own creative horizons and then from that pool of personal growth feed those around you.

Creativity does not spring up from nothing. It has a foundation and a structure within which it lives. A sort of emotionally safe incubator where people are free to experiment, make mistakes and explore free from shame or condemnation. It is like the moisture that gathers from the farthest reaches of an immense watershed that collects and flows into a mighty river. Your job as a project manager/leader is to steward that pool of creative moisture as your natural resource and watch it collect and grow as naturally as water flows from the top of our mountains to the plains.

WARNING

I was at a meeting of project managers last week (taking a break from writing) and a retired PM made a snide remark about creativity and project management. He is an old school engineer who deeply believes that you should know everything prior to starting a project and then drive it to completion regardless of the impediments. It is as if you need to park your creativity hat at the door when you enter the project management arena. It is not needed or wanted.

I was taken aback by his attitude and the certainty with which he held his opinion. I also felt sorry for him. Project management is a great profession and a lot of fun when you have a good objective and a great team. Adapting and adjusting to the cultural and economic tides is part of the deal, a known reality. Creativity and innovation are not luxuries that we pull out during lessons learned or for planning the office Christmas party. They are core drivers in finding success regardless of industry or style of project.

That being said, you do not throw engineering rules and limits away just because you are being creative. Many times deep, profitable innovation comes from defining the limits within which your creativity must live. A great example of this in operation is the LEGO Group in Denmark. LEGO was named the toy of the century in 2003 just as they were going through a financial crisis that almost wiped out the company. They got in the bind via unbounded expansion of creativity. To turn the company around they narrowed and redefined where they could be creative and yet remain profitable. They returned to their simple, constrained and very creative roots. David Robertson in his book about LEGO *"Brick by Brick"* states it this way; "The notion that a company should focus its resources on a clearly defined core business runs counter to much of the prevailing thinking about innovation, which holds that talented associates should have a broad canvas for creativity and be allowed to search for 'blue ocean' markets or develop 'disruptive' technologies … But Godtfred <the founder of LEGO> found that the LEGO System was flexible enough to allow a great deal of innovation within a very tight set of constraints."

They had to return to a narrow focus and distinct limits. Within this box they found ways to regain profitability and remain in that position to this day. They stayed on the page but colored outside the lines. You will see more of this story in this book.

Our hope is that you enjoy this book but also that by reading it and applying some of the ideas, you will improve yourself as a leader and free up the creativity of your team. Begin by coloring outside the lines yourself and then free your team to do the same. Results will be above and beyond anything you have ever experienced before. We know because it has happened to us.

Ted

If you Can't Win the Game...

On Competition and Changing the Way You Look at Business

Recently, I sat down to play a Chutes-and-Ladders-type game with an eight-year old. It was a lot of fun to see her little mind at work, but she had one annoying peculiarity: she was continually bending the rules, reshaping roles, changing the boundaries, reversing strategies. Everything I took for granted, she challenged. Cheating? I don't think so.

When we decide that we are in competition, we implicitly agree to play the game the way it has always been played, to abide by the formal and informal rules and roles, as well as the unspoken rituals. Although competing can be fun and exciting, it is not very creative and definitely limits the imagination. It is because of this experience that I have concluded that *competition encourages conformity.*

Kids are always changing the rules and the way the game is played. Research shows that kids spend more time creating and re-creating a game than actually playing it. So, why not ignore the competition—and start to re-create the way the "Project Management Game" is played??

When you compete head-on, you are just agreeing to play by the old rules...to conform to the way it has always been done...to stay in the lines! Innovation simply means to change the way we do things. I believe that *'There is no such thing as a new idea—only new ways of presenting old ones.'* This hits at the very core of our business persona. Once you make the decision not to "compete", but to define your own market, you can find solace in the fact that you don't have to "re-invent the wheel" to be successful. Approach your opportunity with the mindset that you are simply going to find new ways to present what you already have. Maybe that means simply presenting your service, your product or yourself differently than everyone else.

When you begin to accept competition as a head-to-head battle, then there are no winners and you tend to lose any advantage you ever had in your marketplace. Look at what has happened with airline frequent-flier programs. What was once a very unique, innovative idea now has been copied so many times that no airline has the advantage in this arena. As a matter of fact, I would venture to guess that there is many an airline executive who rues the day that the concept of frequent flier bonuses was ever developed.

It would be naive and foolish of me to say "Don't compete". I realize that anything you can do nowadays to beat your competition to the punch, can give you some small advantage in the marketplace. Though you will gain one-time "one ups" on your competitors by facing them head-on, competing will never present the breakthroughs that you are going to need to really move ahead of the pack nor the staying power you need to survive in any business.

Remember, every new and innovative idea in any business has always—ALWAYS—broken with tradition. I am always preaching about taking a new perspective of the opportunity you have been presented and of the risk you have already chosen to take by doing what you do.

This is not the way your business has been conducted in the past. I have enjoyed challenging many businesses to *"stop looking in their rear view mirrors to see how it has always been done in the past. Start looking through your windshield to see what is coming down the road ahead of you. If you spend your time considering the way*

things have always been done in your profession, you are not prioritizing your energies.

Start asking yourself, *"How can I present the (*fill in the name of your organization here*) 'experience' differently than all the others professing to be in the project management space?"*

I am not suggesting that you don't study what has and hasn't worked for those who have been successful in your business in the past. Quite the contrary! I believe that you have to understand and imitate those strategies that work. It's not until you understand these strategies that you can begin to look for other opportunities to present what you do differently so as to attract customers and sell more.

By changing the rules to the game, you get outside of your comfort zone and begin looking at volatile business challenges from a whole new perspective. We are not going to be comfortable any longer and we can either accept the challenge or get left behind. Wayne Gretzky, one of the all-time greatest hockey players, was once asked by a reporter how it was that he always managed to be where the puck is. With much thought, Gretzky replied, *"I'm not always where the puck is. I am always where the puck is going to be!"*. Are you where your business <u>IS</u> or are you where it is going to be???

Helen Keller once said, *"The most pathetic person in the world is someone who has sight but has no vision"*.

Rather than looking at the competition that *IS*, why not start to create what *ISN'T*?

It still starts with you. What is your mindset and how do you translate that to create a high-performing environment for every project you come in contact with?

Michael Jordon is considered by many people to be the greatest basketball player of all time (sorry LeBron), but he was a part of losing teams until Phil Jackson became his coach. He sat Michael down and explained that he could be the greatest player who ever lived according to statistics or he could create a championship team, but he could not do both. Michael chose to become the team leader and invest in the relationships off the court and on the court that would lead to a championship culture. He changed his vision. You can change your vision as well. Learn to be a leader that creates a high-performing culture of exponential success. Develop your own creativity and innovation quotient and pay attention to what your team members need to do the same thing. Lead out of what you own—your own focus and vision. Set yourself apart from the normal, pedestrian project management herd by clearly identifying the mission and vision of your project and then articulating it in new and creative ways. Choose to become a creative, innovative champion and craft a creative championship culture. Your team will love it, your organization will love it and by the way … you will love it too. Our hope is that this book will spark a few ideas that will help you toward that goal.

Lessons from the Pump

Do people go Out of Their Way to do Business with You?

On a business trip to Washington, DC, I experienced one of those days where everything went wrong from beginning to end. Not only were the day's business dealings a complete flop, but the 250 mile drive back to Pittsburgh PA looked like it was going to be a disaster as well. As I approached the halfway point—an exchange on the Pennsylvania turnpike called 'Breezewood'—I glanced at my gas gage and realized it read empty. I decided to treat myself and I pulled into a full-serve bay; a luxury of which I rarely partake, nor one that you find is offered very often!

Before I could even get my car into park, a young man of about 14 years, threw open the service station door and ran to my car in the pouring rain. I repeat—HE RAN TO MY CAR! From under the brim of his oil stained and rain soaked ball cap, his eyes gleamed and he smiled as he greeted me.

"Hiya sir! Can I help you?"

I was in no mood to be friendly. *"Just fill it up"*, I said rather flatly.

As he approached the rear of my car, he began to whistle loudly. Now, understand that it was freezing outside, this kid is getting soaked and he is whistling. I looked in my rear view mirror and panicked as he proceeded to jam my gas cap into the nozzle to make the gas empty into my car on its own accord. Why the horror? I realized that this left him free to come back up to talk to me. I didn't want to talk to this kid—he was a little too friendly for me.

"So, havin' a bad day are ya?" he deduced. *"What do ya do for a livin'?"* I wasn't going to get into training and consulting with a 14 year old, so I proclaimed myself a motivational speaker.

He smiled a knowing smile and proclaimed, *"SO AM I"*!!!

NOW HE HAD MY ATTENTION. I immediately asked, *"How are you a motivational speaker"*? He looked me straight in the eye and explained, *"Well, I'm not really a speaker, but I <u>am</u> motivational!"* He continued, *"Isn't your job to get in front of people and get them up and going?"* I nodded in agreement. *"My job is to stick the nozzle in and keep them going!!!"*

I would agree that his answer was a little bizarre. This young kid had taught me two very valuable lessons in life. The first is simply to look at what you do from a different perspective. The second, and most important, is that people want to do business with people who seem to enjoy what they do for a living. This kid obviously enjoyed what he did for a living and for the past few years I stop at that gas station in hopes of getting that kid to pump my gas. And the sad thing is that he doesn't even work there anymore. He's in college. I'm just hoping he will graduate and come back to pump gas!!

Do people go out of their way to do business with you? Is the experience such a memorable one that they will keep coming back?

The salient point for project managers from this chapter is, "Your attitude can impact your results".

This is true in relationship to your team but also to the Executive layer and all other relevant stakeholders. The story of this lad who understood in a different light what he was doing in his job can be a motivation to step back. Review what you are doing. Know the significant 'why' for yourself and every other stakeholder. Once you have this understanding, look for an analogy or statement that can reflect this to yourself and any stakeholder or team member. This young man was enthusiastic and stated the truth of his situation in a way that caused Jeff to pause and reflect. The boy was in the motivation business as well and "filled people up to keep them going".

The positive result? Jeff returned to that station, intentionally, multiple times after the first encounter just for the chance of bumping into this 'fellow motivation-delivery' guy. Be upbeat and know your why. Let it seep into the DNA of your life and strong, positive things will occur. Also, people will want to return to your station. When they do, remember to fill them up and keep them going.

The Rock

As Long as Your Goal Doesn't Change and They Use the Tools You Give Them—

Who Cares How they Get There??

In another lifetime—and I don't mean a "Shirley MacLaine" other lifetime—I was a manufacturer's representative. One year, the powers-that-be of the company I represented, decided to get creative. Instead of bringing all of the territory managers to the factory to see the new line of goods, they decided to subject us all to an Outward Bound experience.

For those of you unfamiliar with this, Outward Bound has numerous locations and offers a leadership/team building experience based around a certain activity

11

depending on where in the world it is located. The Outward Bound program in which we participated, was based in Leadville, Colorado, and was centered around rock climbing.

Please understand that, in my lifetime, I never had any ambition to climb a ladder for fun, never mind a large rock! But it was one of those things where the company said "be there" and you had better show. For the first five and one-half hours on the first day, they took us out and positioned the first four of us at the base of a sheer ninety foot rock face and proclaimed, "*You are going to climb to the top*".

This may not sound like a lot of rock to some of you, but just imagine nine stories of jagged rock rising straight above you. I needed more of an incentive than some guy just telling me to climb the rock…so I made one up!

I turned to Craig on my left and challenged him. "*I'll bet you twenty-five dollars I can get to the top first*", I proclaimed. Craig didn't hesitate. "*You're on*", he said confidently. I hadn't even considered my other two colleagues on my other side, but they chimed in that they were in the race as well. Now it was nine stories of rock worth a hundred dollars! I had my incentive.

Each one of us had an individual guide from Outward Bound. I will never forget Joe, my rock climbing mentor, because, at that point Joe whispered in my ear; "*For fifty bucks, I'll get you there first*"! I guessed that this was the teambuilding that they referred to in the brochures! I shook on it.

Joe took me aside and explained in a whispered tone, *"Don't let the others hear. Do you see that rock sticking out at about two and a half feet?"* I nodded. *"When you start, stick your right foot on that ledge and boost yourself up. Next, see that rock, right here at eye level? Grab that rock with your right hand and pull yourself up. The secret to winning, Jeff, is that branch without any leaves on it, at about twelve feet. Grab that branch with your left hand and pull yourself up. It will hold your weight—I've done this a thousand times before."* And, so went the verbal tour up the rest of the rock face.

Someone yelled *"GO!"* I stepped on the rock with my right foot. I pulled myself up with my right hand. I reached out for that naked twig and couldn't reach it. No matter how hard I tried, I couldn't reach it. At that point, my new partner yelled at me, *"Grab the stupid branch"*. Straining, I replied, *"Joe, I can't.......I'm going to die!"*

Please understand that I was only two and one half feet off the ground. I had one foot still on the ground. But, I was going to die!

As I was reaching for that branch, I found a rock sticking out at about ten feet that was easier to seize. As I tested it, I found that it would hold my weight, so I pulled myself up. As I did, Joe yelled at me again. *"No. No. No.*

That's not right." Through clenched teeth, I retorted, "*It's right for me, Joe*".

He yelled at me the entire way up the face of that rock. Did I make it to the top? Absolutely! Did I win? Absolutely not! I am still bitter about that.

What does this experience have to do with creativity-in-business? Everything!

I learned a very valuable lesson while clinging to that rock and being harangued by Joe. As long as I had the knowledge I needed, as long as I used the tools he gave me (ie. the belays—the ropes), and as long as the goal (getting to the top of the rock) didn't change, WHO CARES HOW I GET THERE?

So many organizations with whom I have worked feel it necessary to micro manage every project. If you would simply educate your team, give them a clear understanding of the goals and present them with the right tools, WHO CARES HOW THEY GET THERE?

I encourage you to listen to your environment for whispers of opportunity. Your customers—the people on your team or your external ones—are telling you the second right answer to reaching your goals, if you would just listen!

This Chapter brought back some memories for me. When my oldest son, Benjamin, was thirteen, I took him on an adventure weekend to go whitewater rafting and rock climbing in the wilds of southern Pennsylvania. During the rock climb, Ben was the first person to face the 40 foot rock face. He got about 15 feet up the embankment and froze. He was obviously strapped into a safety harness and yet he was not comfortable going further so we talked him down and the next person up began their assent.

The next person was a fifty year-old woman and she struggled but went all the way to the top and was pumped about the experience. This jolted Ben's thirteen year-old manhood and before I could object, he began free climbing the wall. He went up fast and in no time was at the top waving his arms in victory. His father nearly had a stroke. (How do I explain a broken son to his mother if he fell?). We had a little discussion about safety and having fun responsibly and the medics took care of me!

My point? Jeff's Rock Chapter reminded me once again how we often look at circumstances and determine "We can't do that", or "That isn't possible" even though there may be another option or another way. By simply marshalling ahead, we may find that the obstacle was not as insurmountable as we had assumed.

Jeff's point in this Chapter is "who cares how we get there" which is sound advice many times (unless you have a thirteen year-old daredevil on your crew). My last point is to step back from your wall. Take some time and look for creative alternatives, alone or with your team, and options you never thought of may get you to the top.

The Opportunity

Reframing Your
Professional Problems

I remember calling my office one day when I was in the advertising business. At the time, we had seven or eight account representatives and I recall speaking with all of them on the telephone. After the niceties were out of the way, they all started with the exact same four words: *"I have a problem."*

> *"Jeff, I have a problem with an order."*
> *"Jeff, I am having a problem with a client."*
> *"I have a problem with the receptionist"*
> *"I have a problem with the computer."*
> *"I have a problem with the toilet."*

I got very sick of the word *'problem'*. Think about it. If you have a problem, you automatically have an obstacle to get over. So, in all of my wisdom, I went to our regular Monday morning meeting the following week and challenged everyone to come up with another word to replace the word "problem."

They did it. They decided on the word "Situation". That week when I called in, I heard things like,

"Jeff, I have a *situation* with the receptionist"
"Jeff, I have a *situation* with the toilet."

I felt more like the commander of a naval ship than the owner of my own business. Back to the drawing board.

The following week they came up with a word that has literally changed the way we do business. The word? *Challenge!*

I know you know the word, but why is it that we won't use it? I have a theory. I think human beings love to have problems. I am not trying to be facetious. I think we rely on it as a great excuse. You see, if the problem is big enough, the obstacle is big enough. And, if the obstacle is big enough, the excuse is justified. I've heard it again and again.

"Sorry boss. Too big an obstacle. I tried but I just couldn't get it done."

Instead, why not change it to the word "challenge"? From every problem comes an obstacle. From every challenge comes an opportunity. So, if we can discover the challenges we face—personally or professionally—we can discover the opportunity it presents to us.

"There is more than one solution to any problem."
"Your problem is not your problem; it is the wrong problem."

Dr. Daniel Burrus
from a presentation in Grand Rapids Michigan March of 2014

Jeff's point in this short chapter is that your mindset can limit your creativity. In other words your starting point becomes your ending point. If you think you can or if you think you cannot you are correct.

My wife of 41 years, Claudia, has used an effective phrase for years in our home, "Have another thought". It is how she changes the mindset of a situation and forces alternatives to rise. It made for some interesting discussions over the years in raising four amazing children and it continues to inform our interactions to this day.

I quote Dr. Burrus above because his book "Flash Foresight: How to See the Invisible to Do the Impossible" is a remarkable treatise on how our thinking can limit us or propel us to amazing new heights. We can choose which result by simply changing how we approach problems. His seven triggers that help you see hard trends versus soft trends in any situation will revolutionize how you conduct project planning and problem solving. Never let a problem stop you. There is always another way to look at it.

I quote my brother Dan in our book "The Nehemiah Effect" as saying "we never have problems, we only have opportunities!" If you take another thought about any difficulty or obstacle you face in delivering your projects end goal it will open up fresh ideas. If on the other hand you start with a focus on the problem and its negative implications (or let your team digress into negative discussions regarding the situation or the people involved) instead of opening up the discussion to the possible opportunities the challenge presents, you will not find solutions. You will, however, succeed at draining all of the energy out of the room.

In some respects it is the same statement Moses made in the Torah to the wandering people in the desert, "I set before you this day life and death … now choose life."

As Jeff suggests, choose opportunity.

The Harvey Principle

How to See Invisible Opportunities

Peter Drucker, management guru, said "THE ONLY WAY TO PREDICT THE FUTURE IS TO CREATE IT".

In these times of turbulent change, you have a unique challenge and a unique opportunity in front of you because you have the capacity to literally create your own future from scratch—literally re-invent it so to speak. You have to do this with your business or your responsibilities… re-invent what you do. In your home or business, the need to shatter old models of doing business, is crucial.

The main principle of creating a more positive, productive and profitable future is something probably fewer than one percent of you–at this point in your career—really understand. I certainly do not mean to be condescending in any way, but I assume that most of you have probably not taken the time to even consider this. This is a principle that, once you understand it, goes far beyond positive thinking, far beyond goal setting, far beyond any of the traditional rules of success. If you understand and apply this principle, you will never be afraid of the future. You will always know that no matter what happens, you can come out of it profitably and productively.

The number one principle in creating a profitable, productive and positive outcome is what I refer to as the *HARVEY PRINCIPLE!* How many of you remember the imaginary six-foot tall white rabbit, Harvey, from that wonderful, 1950 Jimmy Stewart movie of the same name? It suggested that perhaps *the one with the imagination, the innovative one, was not the crazy one after all.*

We have to learn how to see the invisible; to see the invisible opportunities where other people see only visible limitations. To see the invisible potential of the people with whom we work—to see the invisible ideas that change the world. Your house started as an invisible, intangible, idea in the mind of a single person. That person's ability to see the invisible—what was not apparent in physical form— ultimately produced a structure. Every great invention starts in the mind—in the invisible. Every great project manager sees invisible possibilities—untapped needs— in a marketplace that needs to be served. The most important skill you can learn in creating your own future, is learning the HARVEY PRINCIPLE (like Elwood P. Dowd) and seeing what others cannot.

Fortunately, many of your competitors are suffering from what may be an incurable and deadly disease. This disease is a mental disease—not a physical one—and no one has been known to die from it physically....only financially! It's been known to be hazardous to the financial wealth of many individuals and corporations alike. Never fear! I have been able to diagnose this disease. Maybe you can arrest the symptoms—recognize them within yourself or your organization so you won't have to pay thousands to see a specialist after it's too late for you or your company.

It's caused by a virus called *Pro.Man.P.I.D.S.—PROJECT MANAGEMENT PROFESSIONALS' INNOVATION DEFICIENCY SYNDROME.* ProManPID Syndrome is a mental infliction that will erode your organization's profits very quickly and keep you office-ridden while your competition is feeling healthy and fit.

The Symptoms

What are the symptoms of ProManPID Syndrome? I've discovered seven. As I describe them, see if they apply to you, your organization or someone close to you because you could be responsible for curing this dreadful disease and turn out to be a hero. These are the primary reasons that people are unable to see their "Harvey."

#1 Internal Myopia

Are you all familiar with myopia? What is it? *Near-sightedness*. What happens with Internal Myopia is that you are so focused on the internal aspects of your project or organization—with the business itself—that you can't see the wider environment. You miss what's happening around you by failing to see the big picture. Sometimes we have to step back and look at the big picture. Force yourself to look at other professions or other organizations outside of your industry and ask yourself, "what are they doing that I might be able to adapt for my business?" Realize that merely paying attention to the triple constraints of Scope, Time and Cost even as detailed in the PMBoK will make this disease worse, not better. You must pay very close attention to why any of this matters for your coustomer or your company and translate that knowledge into the fabric and fiber of your entire project. If you do not you will find yourself delivering technical excellence for something that nobody cares about any longer. Things change so keep your eye on the why.

#2 Ostrich Syndrome

Ostriches bury their heads in the sand while they leave another part of themselves exposed! If you have the ostrich

syndrome, you may not simply ignore reality, you may choose to deny it even exits. There are probably some of you who still deny the fact that information technology and the 'cloud' will change the way you do business. There are some people in your industry who also deny this fact. They have ostrich syndrome.

A current project management version of this is the dismissal of Agile practices. Refusing to grow and adapt within the project management space because of attitudes like; "our methods have worked for 25 years–there is no reason to mess with success." For anyone not paying attention, the market is shifting and shifting fast. Certified Scrum Master designations have risen from around 200,000 to over 400,000 in just the past two years. There will soon be more CSMs than PMPs on the street. Do not put your head in the sand. If you have not already done so, start looking into why Agile is so hot in PM and general management circles. Don't leave your tail feathers exposed.

#3 Past-a-Plegia

What this means is paralysis in the past. This is looking in your rear view mirror. "*What was good enough for running my business years ago is good enough nowadays!*" Remember Howard Johnson's hotels and restaurants? By 1975, the Howard Johnson's company had more than 1,000 restaurants and more than 500 motor lodges in 42 states and Canada. Howard Brennan Johnson—son of the original owner took over the reigns at that point and by the late 1980's he attempted to streamline company operations and cut costs, such as serving cheaper food and having fewer employees. It proved disastrous as guests were finding this new era of Howard Johnson's restaurants and motor lodges unsatisfactory, compared to the services they had come to know for years. And, where are they today? Although Howard Johnson hotels do exist in some markets, they are now owned by Marriott! The point is that business today is not the way business has been done in the past, yet I find so many organizations suffering from this syndrome. Little things hang around from the past to haunt us.

Some of this syndrome is embedded in how your organization operates. Kodak, for instance, is an example of this. They were a company that owned the early digital camera patents and yet did nothing with them since physical film was such a huge and profitable portion of their business. They are not doing so well with that business now. If you had been a PM for them, the culture may have killed off your innovation and ideas but you would have been positioned well for your next step once they closed if your approach was one of forward looking innovation and creativity versus keeping your head down and doing as you were told.

#4 Psycho-Sclerosis

If you have had any dealings in health care, you may recognize this symptom. It's also known as "My way or the highway." Today, I hear it manifest itself in organizations in the following ways:

> *"We've never done that before!"*
> *"That's never been done in this profession before!"*
> *"Last time we tried that it didn't work!"*

If you are a manager who exhibits this attitude we strongly suggest you stop. Stop now. Even if you are right you are killing off any hope that a team member or associate will make a suggestion attempt to innovate on your behalf. Nobody, including you, is right all of the time or right about everything. We need everyone firing on all cylinders if we expect to keep up with the blinding pace of change in our current culture.

If you work for a boss who is like this then do whatever you can to protect your team and work hard to demonstrate success. This does not always work because in the end you do not control other people, but you will feel better about yourself and your team will rise up to assist you when they see you are contending for them against the beast.

In today's crowd sourcing, technology dense environments PMs need to be at the leading edge of collaboration using creative innovation methods and tools. And by the way, as Daniel Burrus says on page 16 in *Flash Foresight*, "Embracing change is no longer enough: we need to transform." Trying to control everything will not allow this transformation to occur. On page 169 of the same book, Dr. Burrus states it well, "The way we have always done it is the biggest hurdle we face going forward into a successful future. The real barriers today are no longer technical or material–they are attitudinal."

#5 Feedback Immunity

Do you know anyone who is immune to feedback? Sure. This just doesn't mean personal feedback from a superior or peer but, more important, feedback from the marketplace. There are those who choose to ignore this symptom because they are so married to the success of the idea that they are unable to process the feedback of the marketplace when it doesn't work. Because we live in a 'customer service oriented environment', I think that this symptom has changed. We MUST respond to our customers' feedback BUT we also have to consider how QUICKLY you respond. It can be something as simple as *"How quickly do you return my call when I leave a message on your voice mail?"*

This is one of the beauties and learnings we draw from the Agile community. Rather than setting requirements in concrete and managing change as a negative disruption until the product is delivered at some distant horizon, Agile methods are structured to receive constant customer feedback. From that feedback you then reprioritize the project activities against the highest value that can be delivered (filtered through the project vision) now that the new feedback has been received. Even if you are in a traditional organization without any Agile methods in play you can still benefit from this by scheduling time every week or so to do a team Retrospective. This allows you to get information on what is going well and what is not going so well and to make course corrections as a continuous improvement practice. If you do not know what a Retrospective is, hit a search engine and type the words Agile and Retrospective. You will have enough info to keep you busy reading for a year or two!

#6 Expertitis

This occurs when you know so much about one area nobody can teach you anything new. You become convinced that all the ideas in that area or field have been invented so you might as well not think of any more.

There was a man in the U.S. Patent and Trademark Office who, in 1899 went on a crusade to close the Patent and Trademark Office. He believed everything that was going to be invented had already been invented. Then he proceeded to ride home on his horse!

The other issue here is the Group Think assent to an expert in the room. If the acknowledged expert says it cannot be done then who are we to question killing that idea or direction? Any time you give the power to an expert you close off any chance for innovation and creative solutions. It was said of Ben Franklin that he was so massively productive as an inventor because he had no formal training so he wandered to places and solutions that nobody had ever considered before. Do not let your team's creativity die at the feet of a known expert. Keep your mind open and find ways to engage everyone in the exploration process. Who knows what electrifying piece of information you may find at the end of that kite string.

#7 Failure-Phobia

This is the fear of making mistakes. In his book *Surviving On Chaos,* Tom Peters talks about how "*successful businesses are those who can fail fast and often*". This book was published in 1987 as a wake-up call to business to embrace change because it is here to stay. Following this same line of thought Tom stated at the end of his keynote address at the Leadership Institute Meeting prior to the PMI Global Congress in Phoenix Arizona in 2014, "If you are not going Agile you are dead!" Change is here to stay and if you are afraid to fail you will never explore past the boundaries of your known borders. Coloring outside the lines can be scary but it is a whole lot scarier to stay in the same spot when the world has moved on.

Although most people are afraid of making mistakes, you can never learn anything without making them. Most people are not comfortable with the idea of making mistakes—of failing. I contend that mistakes are a necessary byproduct of the whole creative process and project management needs this process as much or more than any profession. If you live in a culture that punishes making mistakes you will have to be more creative in finding ways to make this work. It is worth the effort. Do not let the "Whack-a-mole" leaders (Whack-a-mole is the game where every time a mole sticks its head up you hit it with a mallet) who disparage or diminish employees for a failure slow you down. I know it is hard to soar with eagles when you are surrounded by turkeys but work at it. Make it work. *Mistakes are opportunities for learning–fail on to the point of breakthrough and success.*

The Cure

There are five steps to curing this syndrome...to seeing your Harvey...to seeing the invisible...to seeing what others are unable to see. These five steps may seem very basic to you at first but, as any professional athlete—any Olympian—would quickly remind you, victory often comes from sticking to the basics.

#1 Learn to See the World Through Your Client's Eyes

I would like to relate a story to you that illustrates this better than I could on my own. It's from a book that many people have forgotten—written in the 1950's by G. Lyn Sumner—called *HOW I LEARNED THE SECRETS OF SUCCESS IN ADVERTISING.* He tells a story that perfectly illustrates how important it is to see the world through your client's eyes. Keep in mind when this was written; it is very dated and not politically-correct! As I share this, think about how you can associate this to your business:

"It makes no difference whether you are using a full page ad in a magazine or a 5 line classified, it is not the space but what you say in that space that determines the success of that advertisement. Let me give you an example: Our maid had left us and as was the custom in Scranton Pennsylvania, Mrs. Sumner resorted to the method that everyone used to get another one. She called up the Scranton Times, an afternoon paper and asked that the following advertisement be inserted in the classified section under HELP WANTED—FEMALE.

> ### "WANTED—Girl for general housework. 727 North Irving Avenue."

The ad ran for 3 days and nothing happened. It was repeated for 3 days more and when still nobody answered it, I made the suggestion that possibly the copy was at fault. Mrs. Sumner said, "All right. You're an advertising writer. If you're so smart, suppose you see what you can do.

I was very professional in my approach. I said it's easy to understand. Here's a solid column of Want Ads all reading the same:

'WANTED..MAID FOR GENERAL HOUSE WORK'.

Suppose there is a maid in all of Scranton, who wants a position or wants to change her position, which one of these ads is she going to read?

Now, let us put ourselves in the position of the maid herself. Every client has some fault to find with the work we are doing. Every maid has some fault to find with her place of employment. And she has in her mind, her own conception of the ideal place in which to work as every client has in their mind their own perception of their own solution to their own problems.

Let us present our home and all of it's attractiveness in terms of those selling points that will appeal to her. So, I prepared a piece of copy that read like this…

"WANTED…girl to do general housework in small, new home in quiet, attractive hill section. All hardwood floors—easy to keep clean. No washing. No furnace to take care of. Nobody sick. Large airy maid's room. House convenient to 2 bus lines. Small family. Good wages. 727 North Irving Avenue."

We placed that advertisement in the Times on a Thursday when most maids have the afternoon off. The first edition went on the stands at 1:00. By 3, the line of applicants had begun to form on our front porch. By 4, buses were erupting maids in groups at our corner. By 5, Mrs. Sumner had made a selection and the appointed one was happily at work in the kitchen a few minutes later getting dinner.

When I came home I got the full story and I proceeded to analyze it. "You see," I explained, "this afternoon dozens of maids, dissatisfied with their jobs read that column of classifieds. And what did they find? They discovered the perfect place to work. The kind of place they'd been thinking and dreaming about."

The trouble was that I didn't let it go at that. Next morning, I went down to the office and told one of the men there what had happened. He looked at me hungrily, "Man! We've been without a maid for two weeks. I wish you'd write an ad for us". I told him that if he would just give me the specifications of his home as a maid's paradise, I'd be happy to. He gave them to me and, of course, by this time I was getting better at this sort of thing. I wrote an advertisement and he put it in the Times the next day.

What do you suppose happened?

Our maid went down and applied for the job!

This story does a great job of illustrating the power of looking at the world through our prospect's eyes. As basic as this sounds most of us do not do it! Most of us have no idea of how our potential customers perceive us, our product or our service. Every morning, take one minute by yourself and imagine you are one of your clients about to do business with you that day. What do they think of when they think of doing business with you? What do they think of when considering working with you?

Do they associate doing business with you as a pain or a pleasure? Are you just another manager or obstacle? Are you a valuable, problem-solving resource on whom they can rely? Are you professional? The key is to do this for each individual customer, client or stakeholder and put yourself in their shoes. Shorten the feed-back loop so you know quickly what is working and what is not working. Clear definitions followed by strong feedback will always improve results.

#2 Understand and Embrace Your New Roles in a New World

Almost five hundred years ago, William Shakespeare wrote "*All the world's a stage. All the men and women merely players. They have their exits and their entrances and each in his time plays many parts.*" Many of us have been playing our 'roles' far too long and in order to create the future, we must re-write our script. I've identified five roles in my one-act play we call the future: one is the lead role and the other four are supporting roles. You must take on these roles in your business if you are to be more successful. The four supporting roles are as follows:

1. *Challenge solver.* You no longer sell ideas or manage projects. You solve people's challenges. You offer an experience. You *look* for specific challenges then find different ways to solve them. Including you team in this pursuit will increase individual satisfaction and intrinsic motivation.

2. *Solution broker.* In other words, you provide solutions. These may be solutions outside your normal realm. Your clients turn to you in this role because of trust and loyalty and they turn to you first. I had a client recently who called me to ask me if I knew a good plumber in our neighborhood. That's the relationship I want with my customers!

3. *Educator or information provider.* With the speed of change, our clients—both internal and external—need to be educated. You can be an invaluable resource for your clients by positioning yourself as an educator and an information provider. The discount clothing retailer Syms, had a great motto by which we should all conduct business: *An educated consumer is our best customer!* Maybe we should adapt this for project management as *"An educated stakeholder is our strongest advocate."*

4. *Communication enhancer.* This is also referred to as communication *facilitator* or communication *re-enforcer* Perhaps your clients simply need you to listen, or perhaps your product or service will help them with their communication challenges.

Now for the lead and the most important role. It's that of **Questioner.**

We must constantly ask ourselves, "What business am I really in? This is not merely at the organizational level, important as that is. It is also at the project level. What is the mission of this project? What business are we in? What business value will we be delivering? I hate to be the one to break the news to you, but most of you are under the influence of some type of business-induced trance! Most of you are having hallucinations! I don't believe that the majority of your answers would be the REAL purpose of your business. None describe what you *really* do for a living or why you get out of bed in the morning and lock yourself in that office for hours at a time.

I think the purpose of all of our businesses is simply to *attain and retain customers*. If you don't create and keep customers, tomorrow you won't be in business. Granted, a lot of project management is dealing with internal customers, but wouldn't you agree that if we don't make them happy, we may not have another project on which to work? Or we may be looking for gainful employment at another organization?

What would happen if you started looking at your primary role in your business, as the provider of ideas? If you don't have customers for whom to provide those ideas and if the ideas don't work for the customers, it won't do you any good. What would happen if you looked at your emerging lead role as becoming a *Customer Attaining and Retaining Agent?* When you think about it this way, several things happen. First of all, you aren't tied to a specific idea or methodology because all you are doing is creating customers and continually filling their needs. If you offer multiple ideas across a spectrum of opportunities, this can be freeing!

Thus, you have five roles. The main role is *customer creating and retaining agent.* The supporting roles are

1. *Challenge solver*
2. *Solution broker*
3. *Information provider*
4. *Communication Enhancer*

Over the next few days, I would like to ask you to really delve into how you can take on each of these new roles in *your* businesses. It would also be a great team exercise to spend a little time reflecting on these roles.

#3 Learn to Listen to the Environment for Whispers of Possibility

Listen to ideas that your environment offers you. When you think about environmental factors that influence your project or your business, you may think of technology, change, diversity, economy, natural disaster, aging of America, pollution, government control, crime, downsizing and so on. But look at these factors from a different perspective. Within each environmental challenge is an opportunity somewhere. You know, if the dinosaurs were able to do an accurate environmental survey, they may be around today! Dinosaur organizations who are unable to analyze their environment and look for opportunities within it, face the same fate as the dinosaurs. We have to ask ourselves, what environmental factors have I been complaining about or ignoring that could present a real opportunity to create and retain new clients? Referring again to Dan Burrus in his book, _Flash Foresight_, he distinguishes between hard trends and soft trends. A soft trend is something that may happen. A hard trend is something that will happen. One known hard trend that PMs need to be aware of is that the baby boomers are turning sixty-five and leaving the work force. This hard trend will affect and impact every organization and project in America in the next few years. Spend some time learning what soft trends and hard trends are currently or going to soon impact your company or project. It will help you move from reactive to proactive to the best state of pre-active.

STEP #4 Learn to Think in New Patterns

Why is it important for an Olympic athlete to practice every day? To get better at it! We seem to take the basics for granted. How many people practice thinking in new ways as a real discipline? Very few. One of the reasons much of our world is in a quandary as to how to solve our many challenges, is because of this inability to think in a new pattern. Einstein said *"Everything has changed except our ways of thinking."* We have to apply the same disciplines in getting ourselves to think in new ways as we do to getting our bodies into shape or in learning to play a musical instrument. So this fourth step in learning to see the invisible, is to make opportunity-finding a habit every day.

(Authors' note: We challenge you to stop reading this book right now. Go to your calendar and block out time to think; to stretch and grow yourself by reading or exploration or a unique activity. You will find yourself filtering current circumstances through the new data and new ideas will rise as a result. This is not theory. This is how we have operated for years and know it to be true. Come back when you are done setting a date with yourself to think.)

Henry Ford said *"Thinking is the most difficult work in the world and that's why so few people ever do it."* Most of us are thinking the same thoughts in the same way every day and that's why we may beat ourselves up for

never having an original thought when we really need one.
That's because we don't PRACTICE thinking.

I have been driven in my passion to find out why
people perceive the world—or the same challenges—in
ways that limit us unnecessarily. I have been on this quest
in trying to discover how it is that we can practice seeing
challenges in new ways...consciously, so that it becomes
a habitual, systematic resource upon which we can call
at any time to see the invisible. So far, I have discovered
that there is one secret at the core of being able to think
in new ways. One secret at the core of all innovation. One
secret at the core of all creative genius. Every creative or
innovative idea is the answer to one or more questions
asked consciously or unconsciously. Therefore, you can
learn to create ideas at will, by learning to ask yourself
the right questions on a habitual basis. It doesn't mean
that we will all become creative geniuses. I do believe that
we all have some natural talents over each other. Some
of you are more naturally athletic than others and some
are more naturally talented in music or math. But we can
dramatically increase our creativity and innovative power
by asking the right kinds of questions on a regular basis...
simply questioning the norm. As we increase our own
creativity and innovation quotient, there will be a trickle-up
effect on your team and organization as well.

SIX QUESTIONS FOR OPPORTUNITY FINDING

If you apply these questions every single day in every
aspect of your world, you find that eventually, (and this

is a gradual progression—it doesn't happen overnight—
it requires some discipline) you can begin to see the
invisible...to even see Harvey!

Here are the questions:

1. What are the emerging industries, markets and
   opportunities who will benefit from my expertise,
   my product or my methodology?
2. What are the greatest frustrations or challenges that
   the people in these emerging markets are facing or
   going to face?
3. What are their most pressing internal and external
   needs?
4. How can what I do help?
5. What else is needed to solve this challenge?
6. How can I position myself or my business as an
   essential challenge-solving resource to these people?

This process looks deceptively simple, but I challenge
you to go through these questions every day for the
next twenty-one days and I will guarantee that you will
see opportunities that you have never seen before.
Brainspark (the act of sparking ideas versus the violence of
brainstorming) with other people outside of your business.
Read books about things you normally wouldn't read. Go
to trade shows that you have no reason to attend. If you
watch *The Today Show*, watch *Good Morning America*.
Stretch your mind in all these different ways because the
more you do that you will find that creative genius is a
matter of taking disparate ideas and putting them together.

The final step in the Harvey Principle may seem like an afterthought, but it is in fact, the most important.

#5 Learn How to Connect the Dots

There's an old Chinese proverb that says, *If you want one year of prosperity, grow grain. If you want 10 years of prosperity, grow trees. If you want a lifetime of prosperity, grow people*!

Ultimately, the success and profitability of your organization, your team, is only as good as the people in it. You started by offering an opportunity for someone else to possibly change their lives. If you aren't helping those people to grow, if you are not constantly learning and growing: if you aren't caring and compassionate to your people: then ultimately you can't win the game. You know this or you wouldn't be in the business you are in but you have to consistently make it a priority to be successful.

You commit to connecting the dots when you commit to the development of everyone with whom you come in contact.

You commit to connecting the dots when you make a total commitment to absolute equality within your team. You commit to connecting the dots when you commit to keeping ethics above all else.

You commit to connecting the dots when you take care of yourself mentally, physically, spiritually and yes, financially.

You commit to connecting the dots when you commit to nurturing human potential in all aspects of your business.

I want you to take a few minutes over the next couple of days and ask yourself, "How can I bring more caring, compassion and character into *every* aspect of my professional life?" This will get you started on your commitment to connecting the dots.

I want to share a poem with you that I 'massaged', loosely based on one called THREADS written by James Autry. Mine is called Connecting the Dots.

CONNECTING THE DOTS

Sometimes you just connect with an internal or external client...in an instant.

No big thing maybe, but something beyond just a beginning and end of a project...

It comes and goes quickly so you have to pay attention.

A change in the eyes when you ask about their family, a pain flickering behind the statistics about their boy or girl in school far from home.

An older colleague talks about his bride with affectation after 25 years

A hot-eyed achiever laughs before you want him to

Someone tells about his wife's job and how proud he his of her.

A woman says she spends a lot of salary on an day care and a good one's hard to find, but worth it.

LISTEN! LISTEN AND CONNECT THE DOTS!

In every conversation with your clients, you hear the dots of love the dots joy, the dots of fear and guilt, the cries of celebration and re-assurance and somehow we know that connecting those dots is what we are supposed to do and business will take care of itself.

If It Is Broke, Don't Fix It...Yet

Stop Trying to Solve Your Clients' Challenges Too Quickly

Quite awhile ago, I read the book by John Grey, '*Men are from Mars, Women are from Venus*'. I have to admit that it wasn't because I was particularly interested in better understanding my relationship with my wife, but because it was presented to me by my mate as a '*wonderful tool in my business*'. Either way, she got me to read it.

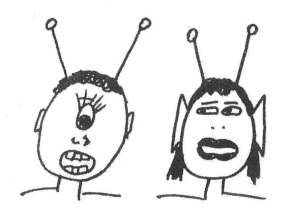

Although now out-dated because of the advancement of male-brain/female brain research, the overt message of the book is that men and women speak different languages. Men speak Martian and women speak Venusian. Whether or not you have read the book, you know this to be true. My wife arrives home and exclaims, *"This house is a mess!"* What's she really saying? *"This house is a mess!"* But, what do I hear? *"Did you make this mess, you slob? Pick up this stuff before I get really angry!"* It's that guilt thing guys!

Much of the message of male versus female communication is stereotypical. Today, much research has been done on "male brain versus female brain", so Grey's book has been de-bunked by many groups but, there is an underlying message in Grey's book that really got me pondering the creative process in any project. That message is that *men won't listen.* Unfortunately, most males also know this to hold true. We want to fix things; it's just our nature. Many woman, on the other hand, just wants us to listen. A while ago, my wife came home from work looking frustrated and explained that she had just experienced *"the worst week of work in her entire life."* Without hesitation I looked at her as empathetically as I could and said *"Quit!"* As if that wasn't bad enough, I was dumb enough to follow this with, *"What's for dinner?"* Not the makings of strong communications in any relationship.

I'd like to write a book called, *"Project Management Professionals are from Mars. Everyone Else is from Venus".* Because of the nature of the beast, you have been trained to fix things. In a recent workshop, I asked project management professionals what was one benefit they offered their clients. 90% of respondents said that they are in the business of solving their clients' problem...of fixing things.

Rumor has it that the leading manufacturer of typewriters back in the 1880's was approached by Remington Inc. to sell their company. Remington, however, commented that it would not make an offer until the original company solved a serious problem that had been uncovered. Remington had discovered that typists were complaining that the keys of the typewriter were sticking.

Now, I remember as a kid, having to reach in and undo stuck typewriter keys, so it must have been a lot worse back at the turn of the century. Keep in mind that the keyboard configuration did not look anything like it does today. In this instance, the top row was capitals, the second row was small letters, the next was numbers and the bottom row was punctuation. Finally, the letters were arranged alphabetically and the keys were about double the size they are now.

The president of the original company got his bigwigs together and challenged them to solve the problem. To their credit, they did not jump to the solution too quickly. They did something that hits at the very core of creativity and is my motto in business today. *"When you have a problem, BLAME THE CUSTOMER!"* Now, don't do this out loud, but it truly helps to take the blame off of your people and put it elsewhere. So, the typewriter executives said, *"It's not our fault the typewriter keys stick. It's the typist's fault—they're typing too quickly."* From this, the company's engineers came up with the most inefficient keyboard system they could dream of. It's called QWERTY (the first six letters of your keyboard) and we still live with it today.

Think about it. The I and the O are the third and sixth most frequently used letters in the English language. Where are they located? Top right and probably your weakest fingering. The new configuration did slow down typists and the company was sold to Remington! I don't want you to rebel against typewriters, but I do want you to hesitate before you just try to fix your clients' challenges. Maybe we need to re-evaluate the problem before jumping to the solution too soon. By doing this, we set ourselves apart from our competition by exhibiting more professionalism and innovation.

"Festina Lente–Make haste slowly", Latin Proverb
"Slow down to go fast" Japanese Proverb
My point in starting this chapter summary with a Latin Proverb is not to show off the skills developed in my 9th grade Latin class (Mrs. Brown passed me only due to my good vocabulary scores). My point is to highlight the fact that some words of wisdom resonate through the ages ... and yet we still do not pay attention to them.

Does this scenario sound familiar... You just finished your project and the next project is handed to you; behind schedule, over budget, poorly defined and in a swirl? What do you do? Many times the first reaction of the project manager (encouraged by senior management) is "Don't just stand there, do something!" Unfortunately this is exactly the point to stop any actions perceived to move the project forward.

This is the time to stop and begin asking questions; for example "Why are we doing this project?" "Who benefits and why should we care?" "Who else has done a similar thing before and can we chat with them?" I am sure you can quickly come up with a strong list if you try. Forcing a "Stop the engines!" moment to access the project in light of the overall mission of the organization and understanding the compelling "whys" will allow you to aim at the right things even as the project landscape morphs and changes during the project execution process. The Remington engineers solved 'a problem' but the downstream loss in productivity long after sticky typewriter keys are a dusty memory.

The re-evaluation suggested by Jeff is awesome. This should be done through the lens of the organizational Purpose, Mission and Vision and that each change to the eventual plan has to be again accessed through the same lens.

The other point here is that sometimes, to go faster, you have to go slower. You have more planning and process work to do if you want delivery to be fast. You may have seen on YouTube the time-lapsed video of the 19 story building in China that was erected in three days. Pretty cool. What they don't show in the video are the months and months of process honing and practice that allowed that team to deliver its "fast" project.

Ask the right questions, solve the right problems and slow down to go fast. Sounds like good advice to me.

Step Into My Office

Shattering the Stereotype of Doing Business With You

I was driving my rental car along Northwest Highway in Dallas. I had about three hours to kill prior to my scheduled flight at DFW airport. I turned a corner and there in front of me was a building with a sign, *"DALLAS FINE CARS... Luxury Automobiles at Their Best."*

I have never taken time to stop to look at these high-priced indulgences. I hear this mid-life crisis thing is coming, so my wife tells me it's OK to look at sports cars... as long as that's all I do!

I pulled into the parking lot, got out of my car and peered through the window of the showroom. There, in the middle of the showroom floor (on a pedestal), was the biggest, the blackest, the most beautiful Mercedes Benz I have ever seen in my entire life. At that moment, all I wanted to do was sit behind the wheel of that car and fantasize that I owned it.

Before I go any further, do we have a stereotype of the 'typical' car salesperson? Absolutely! You may be married to one. You may have had a great experience with one, but overall, we still have a vision of the stereotypical car salesperson in North America. I am aware that many car dealerships are working on this image, but the fact remains that this impression is still not a good one.

Adjectives such as *sleazy, slick, dishonest, aggressive, pushy and Herb Tarlick* still roll off of most peoples' tongues. I have the same stereotype plus the amazing realization that this is the one industry with whom I have worked, in which they can't sell you their product! Ask a car salesperson for their card. Their title is likely to be "Sales Associate" or "Salesperson". Then you get to the point when you want to buy the car and they panic…"Oh, wait! I have to get my sales manager." They can't sell it to you!

So, I have the same stereotype as most others as I push open the door of the car dealership. Before I could even get through the doorframe, my stereotype was completely shattered. Why?

A woman approached me. Now, I would venture to guess that even if you are a woman, you wouldn't have thought of a woman when I asked you to stereotype the typical car salesperson. We think of a man.

This was great. My stereotype was completely shattered as a woman approached...but she didn't let me down. You can guess the first words out of her mouth. In any retail situation, what do we get asked the most? *Can I help you?* And, what is our defensive answer—whether we mean it or not? *"No thanks. Just looking."*

This is a pet peeve of mine. If you have any responsibility over this in your business, think of something besides asking, *"Can I help you?"* It's like getting your swords out. Imagine two people facing each other. The first yells, *"Can I help you?"* while drawing their sword. In response, the second waves his sword while proclaiming, *"No thanks. Just looking."* Not to be daunted, dueler #1 jabs his sword while asking, *"What can I show you today?"* In a final display of showmanship, dueler #2 strikes back with *"Nothing! I am just looking."* OK. Maybe I get carried away, but that's just how bad I think it is to ask this meaningless question.

Back to the car dealership...when we had last left our hero (me), I had just begun jousting and had sternly reported that I was just there to look. Without another word, the woman looked me in the eye and ordered, *"Step into my office!"*

I thought I was hearing things. I could have sworn she had just <u>ordered</u> me into her office. I was still standing in the doorframe. The look on my face must have betrayed my confusion. Without hesitation, she repeated, *"Step into my office,"* as she turned her back and walked away.

I conduct some sales training, but I don't need another case history. After the shock wore off, I decided it was time to hightail it out of there. As I turned to leave, I glanced over my shoulder one more time. Do you know what she had done? She had walked swiftly to the back door of that black, Mercedes Benz—at which she must have seen me looking in the window when I first arrived. She opened the back door of the car, slid into the back seat and, with a smile on her face, she now yelled at me—through 2 open doors—*"Step into my office!"*

I was back! Oh, come on. It's been a long time since I was in the back seat of a car with a woman. And, my wife will tell you, it was never a Mercedes Benz!

How odd is this? I now find myself sitting in the back seat of the car with this salesperson, when she barks another order. *"Shut the door."* I comply.

Without hesitation (and I have now totally given over control to her), my new friend looks at me mischievously and tells me to smell. Not sure that I heard her correctly, I ask her to repeat the command. She repeated, *"Smell."*

"Shouldn't we introduce ourselves first?" I try to stall.

"Just smell." She is getting impatient.

As I take in what I can using my olfactory senses, I find myself overwhelmed with the smell of leather. I relate this to the young woman.

"That's what your kids are going to smell when they are sitting in these seats," she explains.

All I could say was a very profound *"WOW."* She had me now.

Next, she asked me to look around the front seat and report what I saw. I observed a leather-bound steering wheel and wood paneling. When I was done reporting, she explained, *"That's what your kids are going to see when you are driving this car!"*

Again, all I could utter was, *"WOW!"*

"Sir, do you like to go fast?" she teased. *"Yeah, really fast,"* I mumbled. *"This car is the fastest car on the lot,"* she explained boastfully.

Another *"WOW".*

Next came an invitation. *"Imagine your hand on that stick shift; shifting from fourth into fifth at eighty to eighty-five miles an hour."*

"WOW"

Then came the kicker. *"Do you have the money?"*

"No," I replied honestly.

She politely excused herself to go shock another potential customer!

This whole experience completely shattered the stereotype of the <u>experience </u>I expected to have walking in those doors.

Do your clients have a stereotype of the experience they are going to have with you? Whether it's a prospect or someone on your team, we must constantly figure out ways to shatter the stereotypes that they have of us, our product or service, or of doing business with us. Perhaps it's physically changing the environment or surroundings in which you have your parties or your presentations. Maybe it means holding that weekly Skype™ meeting from a different venue. You could simply change your voice mail message or your signature at the bottom of your email.

One enterprising project manager with whom I have worked took my advice to heart. Each week she held a combination update and motivational call. She had been conducting conference calls for years and she related how she had recently switched to video meetings. She also told me that it had changed her business. Each week, she holds her call from a different venue which she can use as an example of great service or successful business techniques or for just a great experience. These have ranged from Starbuck's to Chucky Cheese to her car dealership.

Do whatever it takes to first understand the stereotypes that exist in the project management profession and then shatter them…creatively!

> "The single biggest problem with communication is the illusion that it has taken place."
>
> George Bernard Shaw
>
> What Jeff encountered at the car dealership was not a failure to communicate but the utilization of excellent multi-sensory communication tools to lure him into purchasing a car. We in the project management profession should take notice.
>
> Communication is not just the Encode–Send–Noise–Reciever and back path that we learn in the PMBoK. It is the engagement of all the senses to make sure that the person recieving the message indeed 'gets it'. This is one of the reasons I love Agile project mangement frameworks like Scrum. It uses physical Kanban boards to engage sight. The individual team members phisically move their stickies from backlog (Agile's version of a Work Breakdown Structure) to Doing to Done so touch is engaged. The various structured meetings facilitate conversations that engage the entire group and garner feedback in and insight from all team members and relevant stakeholders. I beleive it is one of the core reasons these methods work. They are multi-dimentional.
>
> You may not be able to take your stakeholder out to an automobile dealership so you can "invite them into your office" but I daresay you can creatively come up with a number of ways to fully engage all of their senses

in how you present and gain reaction from the items you are trying to communicate in your project.

A great exercise would be for the team to come up with ideas on how to facilitate this. Any small step you take in this direction will cause your project communications to improve.

The saleslady knew what the "wow" was. Experience the car and imagine yourself in it. Strive to create a "wow" effect every time we engage with a project or project team. Try to identify what will cause the sponsor or key stakeholder to go "wow, that is amazing!"? That is the effect you are looking for and want to draw them into ... the same way Jeff was invited to get in the car.

This is not new, by the way. An offical in the court of a Babalonian King obtained this response from the locals who wanted to kill his project. Their response to Nehimiah's successful project completion was, "Surely their God must be with them!" In other words, you should not have been able to pull that off, we are impressed. That is what we call the Nehemiah effect. An unsolicited "wow" response. You can do the same thing. Take the time to find out what that wow is and aim your team at its delivery.

The Most Powerful Words...

How to Get "Buy In" Once You Are Creative

Let me introduce you to the most powerful words when it comes to success-in-business. To tease you a little, when we first discovered these words in our organization many years ago, they accounted for a 37% increase in business in one year. Not only that, but they completely changed the way we interacted with our internal and external customers: they illustrated how to get "buy in" to our creative ideas. And finally, these two words changed the way I parent my children as well.

Curious? Before I give you the answer, let me explain that this is a process that will help you with recruiting new people and moving your product or service—guaranteed!

It starts with a problem. Remember, in an earlier chapter I explained that you offer solutions. You can't offer a solution if your prospect doesn't have a problem to solve. Also in another chapter, I suggested that our inclination when we hear a problem, is to solve it. Instead, I want you to pose a "What Effect" question.

(prospect) I can't invest in your opportunity. My husband and I agreed not to spend any more money this year.

(you) What effect has spending money had on your family in the past?

Now, just listen. You have just taken things to a whole new level. Your prospect/customer needs to know you are listening. 'What Effect' questions do just that.

In my experience, after asking a 'What Effect' question, you will hear something that starts with, "Now that you mention it…" or "I hadn't really thought about it but…" All you've done is taken this a step deeper than most people instead of trying to solve it.

The next step is using the two most powerful words in the English language to let people know that we understand. Empathy is our greatest tool in business today and it's not just good enough to let people know we are listening. The words are "WHAT IF." Allow me to take you through a series of what-iffing that changed the way we did business.

At its very basic level, what-iffing "*shatters the stereotype of the experience your clients expect to have with you.*" (see previous chapter). I must give credit to one of my creativity gurus, Roger von Oech. He is the author of a wonderful book, first published by Warner Books in 1983, *A Whack On The Side of the Head.* In 1986 he published a sequel, *A Kick In the Seat of the Pants* through Harper and Row Publishing. Both are still tremendous books on the whole creative process. Von Oech introduced his readers to What Iffing. I took his suggestion, and began by starting all of my staff meetings with this concept.

Appoint someone the "What-if-questioner" of the day. Their job is to come prepared to kick off the meeting with a bizarre, unreal and totally un-work-related What If question. For example, "What if humans didn't need to sleep?" "What if we had a 12 year old President or Prime Minister?" A client of mine recently tried this and the question was, "What if hair grew inward instead of out?" I have to clear my throat just thinking about it!

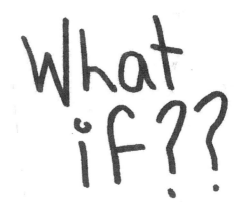

Once the question is on the table, go around the room and make everyone answer it. What's going to happen? One—the creative juices will start flowing and you will be amazed at what evolves. Two—anyone who doesn't normally contribute will be thinking, "Wow, anything I say couldn't be nearly as weird as what just went on here!"

And, three—your people will start to have FUN! Wouldn't you agree with me that people want to work for/work with people who seem to enjoy what they do for a living? As a matter of fact, in all of my consulting, I have discovered a very simple principle...

There is a direct correlation between the amount of fun an organization encourages and the amount of creative breakthroughs that organization experiences.

People are more likely to contribute in an environment that is fun, creative and innovative than in one that is the 'same old, same old."

There is one last saying that should be imprinted in your brain. This is one of those sayings that I have used as my personal creativity mantra for years, but one which I have no idea to whom I owe credit.

There is very little difference between "aha" and "ha-ha"

Then, once you have mastered this internally, try it with your external clients as well.

Let's take What iffing to the next level. Imagine that you now work for me. Let's also suppose that you get to work every morning around nine a.m. I come to you one day and state, "*We have this huge proposal that we have to get done. I can't finish it without your input. I know you normally get here at nine o'clock a.m., but I want you here by seven a.m. tomorrow.*"

How would that make you feel? Not very tactful was it? But, that is basically the way I worked with my people when I first started in business. I thought it was normal—in business—for people to come to work for me for thirty days and leave!!

Then, I discovered what if. Imagine the same scenario: "Hey, you are a huge part of the team and I can't do this proposal without you. I know you normally get here at nine o'clock, but *what if* you came in at seven o'clock tomorrow and get it done?"

At this point, I want to teach you a very sophisticated creativity-in-business concept called '*B.Y.T*" or *bite your tongue*! I can't tell you how many people, with whom I have worked, who ask a question and then answer it. If you ask a question, shut up and listen.

(Employee) *"Jeff, I can't get here by seven because I can't get my kids to the babysitter before seven-fifteen. That means I couldn't be here until at least seven-forty-five."*

(Jeff) *"Could you get here every day this week at seven-forty-five?"*

(Employee) *"Sure. And, if I don't get it done, I could come in Saturday morning…"*

What just happened? I opened up a dialogue; a dialogue that I didn't allow to exist before because of my management style.

I thought, "If this works at my office, this will surely work at home."

We use a disciplinary tactic in our home called "time out". Many of you are probably familiar with this strategy. (My parents thought that *we were* out of our minds. *"Just hit the kid,"* was more their approach to child rearing!) About the time that I discovered "What If", I realized how threatening I must have sounded to my three year old. *"Get into time out and figure out why you did what you just did."* Not much room for discussion.

To this day, no matter how angry I am with my girls, I always start with What If. "What if you went into your room and figured out why you just hit your little sister?" In their minds, it is less-threatening and it opens up a dialog (not that I would listen to a word they say when I really angry!). In fact, now that my oldest daughter is a young adult, she won't hesitate to start the dialog, "I'll tell you why I did it." And we have this amazing conversation that just blows me away. Why? Because when you open up a dialog, you had better be prepared for what you are about to hear.

Finally, let me tie this together by showing you how we made money with What If. I recall a sunny day in 1991, when I returned to a prospect's office to make a creative presentation. Part of my advertising business in those days was devoted to promotional products. This client had given me the challenge of coming up with an imprinted item that would attract people to their trade show booth at various shows around the country. Let me paraphrase the conversation as I recall it…

(Jeff) *"Thanks for meeting with me about your trade show challenge. We spent some time brainstorming, and we think you should give away ceramic coffee mugs"*

Interested nod from prospect encouraged me to continue.

(Jeff) *"We can put your fifteen-color logo on one side and your mission statement on the other. When people come into your booth, fill the mug with water. Attendees will be walking around the show with a cup of water and others will inquire as to where they got it. What do you think?"*

(Prospect) *"Great idea, Jeff. What else did you come up with?"*

(Jeff) "You don't understand. I have been in this business for ten years and I know that this is the answer."

In this scenario, how do we sell our ideas? Like two fists hammering each other and, if I hit hard enough, I win. Now, let's look at the same scenario using what if.

(Jeff) *"Thanks for meeting with me about your trade show challenge. What if you gave away ceramic coffee mugs?"* B.Y.T! Stop and listen.

(Prospect) "Jeff, I can't. I can't ship ceramic across the country because they will break."

(Jeff) "What if we used plastic mugs?"

(Prospect) "Hey, what if we used plastic beer steins? Our theme this year is 'Flow Through Ideas' and a beer stein might get the point across."

(Jeff) "I have a plastic beer stein that, when you put cold water in it, the imprint changes color."

(Prospect) "What if we imprinted it with our old logo and our new logo appeared...?"

Back and forth. Back and forth. When I leave, what does the prospect say to everyone with whom they work? "*I have a great idea and I want to work with Jeff because it feels right.*"

We need to check our egos at the door. I wasn't trying to pull the wool over this person's eyes. I truly believed that ceramic coffee mugs were the "right" answer to her challenge of what to give away in the tradeshow booth. But, if she didn't believe it, it doesn't matter what I think. I walked in selling ceramic coffee mugs. I walked out selling plastic beer steins. Why? Because I opened up a dialogue and somewhere in that repartee, we both agreed that plastic beer steins just might be the second right answer to the challenge of what to give away.

In a previous chapter I said, "*As long as your client uses the tools you give them, and the goal doesn't change, who cares how you get there?*" As long as she used the tools I gave her and the goal—what do I give away in my tradeshow booth—doesn't change, who cares how we got there?

That's the power of what iffing. The results don't come without risk. By opening up a dialogue with your clients, you had better be prepared for where you may go.

But, this all comes with a warning! This is a sequential process and you can't skip any one of the three stages: PROBLEM, WHAT EFFECT and WHAT IF. If you skip to what-iffing without asking a What Effect question, people think that you already had an answer and all you did was put what if in front of it.

Let's look at a simple illustration of all of this. A large firm with whom I have worked, embraced this system whole-heartedly. Their people now start their initial meetings something like this:

(Project Manager) "What are some of the biggest obstacles you face to achieving success in this project?" (stop and solicit responses)

(Project Manager) What effect does not having the financial resources you need have on its potential successful completion? (once again solicit responses)

(Project Manager) What if you had $2,000,000.00 handed to you for this project right now?"

(Stakeholder) "Really? OK. First, I would want to ..."

What will happen is they will begin thinking without putting the lid on and possible solutions will emerge.

What's just happened? As odd as this sounded, it shattered the stereotypical presentation that the stakeholder expected. More important, whether the stakeholder has two million dollars or two thousand dollars, they have just expressed their actual priorities, their hopes and their dreams. Now it is your job to leverage this information to your advantage.

I have been talking about this system for years. Recently I overheard my niece speaking to her daughter...

(neice) Honey, it seems like you had a terrible day. What's going on?

(daughter) Julie told everyone that I liked Todd and that's not even true.

(neice) What effect did that have?

(daughter) Everyone teased me all day and Todd won't even talk to me

(neice) What if you went to Todd tomorrow and told him exactly what happened?

...a great dialogue pursued. The travails of an 11 year old girl!

Many project managers are expected to be on top of all aspects of a project and its deliverables from the moment they are assigned to the day the project is complete. In fact, all too often, they do know more about the overall result and how to get to it than any of the domain experts who are part of the team or are key stakeholders.

This is not a bad situation per se. It can, however, be a source of frustration. This is particularly true when deadlines are looming or costs are suddenly escalating and the world is spinning out of control. Many times, the first intuitive response a project manager has to making a difficult alteration to a project plan is to take an action, any action, to counter any possible negative pushback or results. This approach allows 'cover' should someone question how the team is responding. {When "X" happened we took the following steps to mitigate "Y" and "Z"} is a safer place to be than "we are looking into alternatives."

Jeff's advice in this chapter is actually sound counsel beyond uncovering deeper motivations with prospects whom you are trying to sell. It also makes sense when you are trying to mine different solutions to difficult situations from your team or stakeholders. "What if ..." and/or "What if we ..." are powerful phrases for drawing out ideas and approaches that would go unmentioned without the leadership of a steady, confident project manager.

"Go opposite". "Think top down instead of bottom up" or "Look at hard trends not soft trends and measure true variables not proxy-variables" are all variations of "What if ...". Don't let the urgency of any situation cause you to enter a reactionary state. Step back, facilitate some brain-sparking with your team and then vote (more on dot-voting in a bit) on which idea makes the most sense right now. It will energize the team and bring fresh insights into whatever firestorm happens to be up on your radar today.

To Err is Right...or at Least Necessary

Taking the Fear Out of Being Successful

Most people involved in project management are not comfortable with mistakes. We learn early that it is good to be right and bad to be wrong. These values are all a result of our educational system, which—when you think about it—rewards us by grading the number of right and wrong answers and teaches us that we will be rewarded in life for being right and will have limited opportunities if we make mistakes.

The notion of not being able to make mistakes is still evident in every facet of our adult lives. There are few people who are willing to admit their mistakes in a very public arena. We tend to take risks only on a private level where we feel safe.

This attitude makes sense in many circumstances. You wouldn't want your stockbroker to be wrong too many times. You would assume that the engineer did not make too many mistakes when designing the bridge you drive over ever morning. And, every time you board an airplane, you are betting that the pilot is not overly comfortable with making too many errors.

When it comes to your business however, TO ERR IS NOT WRONG! Mistakes are a necessary bi-product of the creative process. If you are willing to accept the norm because that is the way it's always been done—if you are prepared to sell the same old product or service because it's an old mainstay—then you are not exercising your *"risk muscle"* and your creative genius can only be stifled.

As Benjamin Franklin once said, *"The man who does things makes many mistakes, but he never makes the biggest mistake of all—doing nothing!"*

One of the biggest reasons we don't tend to take risks, when confronted with the many challenges we face, is fear.

Fear keeps us from turning that "one-in-a-million" idea into reality. Fear is the greatest hindrance to successful risk-taking and to performing our best under pressure. To keep ahead of change and to successfully confront the many challenges we face in business, we need to learn how to overcome this obstacle.

The good news about the fear of failure is that we have plenty of company. Everyone is afraid when taking a risk or tackling a new challenge. If you say you have no fears, you are either playing life much too safely or you just are not in touch with your own feelings.

"Heroes and cowards feel exactly the same fear," said Gus D'Amato, the great boxing trainer to such prize fighters as Floyd Patterson and Mike Tyson. But like all champions, D'Amato adds, *"Heroes just react to fear differently."*

One project manager recently said to me, "Hell, making the decision to do this for a living was the scariest thing I have ever done. Picking up the phone to arrange a meeting with someone I don't know is easy-peasy compared to that!"

Fear is like a wall that limits your view and creates boundaries to your growth and, especially to your innate creativity. The successful project manager recognizes that the breakthroughs in their own creative genius, learning and growth, lie beyond the wall.

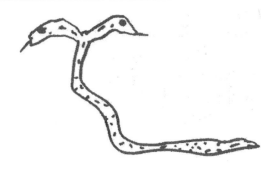

To get over the fear of failure, you must first acknowledge it. There is an old American Indian story that says fear is like a sixty-foot, two-headed snake as big around as a large tree. Avoid it and the snake grows larger and comes closer, rearing its huge, ugly head, ready to strike. But, if you look the snake in the eye, it sees its own reflection, gets scared and slithers away. The next time you face a challenge that requires you to take the risk that you might be wrong—that you might fail—stand up to your two-headed snake of fear.

One entrepreneur with whom I worked, stated that he felt that true risk-taking is for those who have the time and money to do so. Wrong! The truth is that we are all born risk takers. How else do we learn to walk, talk, ride a bike, ski or get ourselves into business?

I am not a scientist, but I would venture to guess that research would show that we learn more in the first decade of our lives than we ever will after that. That's no accident. Isn't this the period that we are more likely to take risks?

If we weren't born risk takers, we would all be crawling around on our hands and knees! *"I don't know if I should try to stand. I'm only a 1 year-old. I will fall. I think I will wait until I am older and stronger."* As children, we don't know any better than to explore the unknown, the untried, the untested every day. This is the prime time for making mistakes, picking ourselves up, dusting ourselves off, and trying again!

It should become evident that you can't learn without taking risks. It's the way we have mastered everything. Growth and creativity come from trial and error. As Lloyd Jones noted, *"The men who try to do something and fail are infinitely better than those who try to do nothing and succeed."*

"*Vulnerability ... the birthplace of creativity, innovation, and trust.*"

Dr. Brene Brown " Daring Greatly

"Fear of failure is failure."

Gen. George S. Patton, Jr.

I agree with the underlying premise of this Chapter immensely.

Project Management is seen as a "construct the rails and stay on the rails you have built" profession and is primarily practiced this way, in my experience. If you want creative go talk to sales or marketing.

The problem with this is two-fold; one, it ultimately ends up costing the organization more and two, it becomes a practice based on fear and the façade of invulnerability.

The first point is easily demonstrated by a simple example. Boeing pushed much of the design decision making on the creation of its 777 jet liner down to the 5,000 engineers working on the various aspects of the new plane. They did this by setting a rule that any engineer could alter his or her design, if it increased unit cost by up to $300.00 as long as it saved at least one pound in weight. They did not need approvals or sign-offs thus streamlining the development process with a side benefit of increasing the job satisfaction for 5,000 people. Many command and control oriented organizations hold control over those types of decisions at higher levels to "make sure" that the highest value is derived from the employee activity. This actually has the opposite effect in that it slows down decision-making and extends the time it takes to get a product to market, and many excellent ideas never see the light of day because they will need someone from 'on high' agreeing that it is a good idea.

This example is found on page 42 of "The Principles of Product Development Flow" by Donald Reinertsen. In discussing this decision by Boeing he states, "The intrinsic elegance of this approach is that the superiors didn't actually give up control over the decision. Instead, they recognized that they could still control the decision without participating in it. Control without participation is control without decision-making delays."

The same positive effect will happen within a project when the project lead allows the team members the freedom to make decisions within their area of expertise. You control the ultimate cost and flow via the rules that set the boundaries of action. If you want examples of this within a project environment go observe an Agile team in action. They are working within specific time boxes and working on the highest prioritized value by working in concert with the Product

Owner to determine what work items (user stories) they are delivering in the very near term. Any leader of any project can realize the benefits that flow from this structure and attitude. Many times the impact and results are immediate.

The second point is wound in with the first point. Most project managers do not like change and do not like to move outside of their comfort zone or as Jeff would put it 'color outside the lines'. They want to make a tight plan and then deliver that plan on time, on scope and on budget. The problem is not that they have a plan, it's that the speed of change in our business and organizational environments today does not lend itself to ridged, immoveable plans that require multiple sign-offs every time a change is made. When traditional approaches compete with adaptive methods the adaptive approaches will win every time. The challenge then is to find ways, even within highly structured or regulated milieus, to push decision-making down to the lowest responsible level. Identify the value, or vision, for which you are aiming and then create rules that free the people delivering the daily tasks to make decisions. Mr. Reinertsen makes a compelling economic case showing that moving decisions to this level optimizes profitability and also frees up creativity and innovation. This is a good thing. But even when these options are given many times the team member or project leader will not exercise them. Why? Fear.

As Dr. Brown points out in "Daring Greatly", fear guts creativity. It takes confidence, courage and vulnerability to operate without fear. But, what if a mistake in judgment is made? Mistakes in judgment happen every day on every project across the globe. Operating in fear, which leads to a lack of vulnerability, is a cultural constraint. If you live in an error-adverse environment then it is very difficult for trust and vulnerability to develop. The issue is that without trust and vulnerability you will never have a high performing team.

If you are a project lead you can create a culture of trust and openness on your team. It takes time to establish this bubble, but the results are exponential. Everyone begins firing on all cylinders and the ideas begin to flow. Will every idea be a winner? No. Will some of the ideas be winners? Without question. This is a true golden nugget for creativity for project managers–form a culture that fosters openness and vulnerability, open up decision-making at the task level and watch creativity flow.

One of the biggest risks a project manager faces is the risk of letting go. Letting the team create, co-create and innovate. Why? It can get messy. But no leader has all the answers, so let go.

86 the Onions

We Need to Stop Being
So Critical of our Own Ideas

In discussing creativity with many project managers around
the world, I have found a real need to get back to basics in
working with the "internal client" in brainsparking new and
innovative approaches to their specific industry.

I would like to clear up some misconceptions about the
very word, '*brainstorm*'. I have never felt comfortable with
this terminology. We are all familiar with one definition of
the word, 'storm' which is an atmospheric disturbance of
some kind. Perhaps this is not far off for some people's
minds, but I don't think that this is what lexicologists had
in mind. I think they were referring to the definition of
storm as "a violent outburst" "to attack or assault". Perhaps
it's the non-violent being inside me, but this seems a
little extreme. For our purposes, I would like to consider
ways to '*BRAINSPARK*'. Simply put, we are in search of
methods and techniques to spark that part of our brain
which will ultimately help us develop new approaches to
old challenges.

Every time you sit down to brainspark, force your group to come up with at least thirty-three different options! Thirty-three different ideas? You don't have the time? Where are you going to find other people with whom to brainspark? How do you do this if you can only come up with ten? Relax!

Human nature prevents us from having an open mind all of the time. We tend to play our own worst critic. If you have ever worked in a restaurant, you are aware of the term '86'. You may have heard the short order cook screaming, *"Order's up! Burger deluxe, 86 the onions"*. It simply means to 'get rid of' or 'scratch'. It's no different in our business lives. We tend to '86' our ideas before they ever have a chance to develop. This is the first reason to force yourself to come up with at least 33 different ideas when brainsparking. We don't have time to 86 our ideas.

At the risk of making you a little schizophrenic, I like to think that we all walk around with two little make-believe 'beings' on our shoulders. On one side we have our internal *Artist* whispering things like, "Go for it" "Give it a try" "What if….". On the other shoulder is our internal *Judge* whispering in the other ear, "Don't take the risk…" "You're an idiot to try it…" "But, it's never been done before". The problem is that too many of us end up listening to our Judge before our artist ever has a chance to finish playing. When it comes to brainsparking for innovative approaches to our challenges, we have to allow the Artist inside to play with the ideas rather than '86ing' them. Think about it. You listened to that Artist when you decided to get into this crazy business, so don't ignore it now!

I first discovered this concept while working as an outside consultant to an architectural design firm in Singapore. One of my challenges was to see if we could come up with a simple name for a small fabric company that the firm was starting as a sideline. While conducting a two-day program with the group of ten on a variety of creativity and vision issues, just before the lunch break on day one, I asked everyone to bring back suggestions of a new name for this company.

When we reconvened after our meal, I brought out my felt tip pen and positioned my flipchart ready to record a series of great suggestions. What I heard instead was ten individual ideas, one per person, even though I hadn't set any limits. All were similar to the company's current name or, even worse, a competitor's. At first, I prevailed on the group to come up with just one more suggestion and with a little struggle, someone did. Better? Yes, but not nearly good enough.

After a few minutes of consideration, I decided to start the process over again with the rule that now the first eleven names were considered off-limits. So I gave everyone a few minutes and asked for a second series of ten. With some struggling we achieved our goal. Now, I challenged the group to find the eleventh and they did. This was the best of the group.

At the end of the day, I assigned the task of coming up with a third group of ten. After all, they would have all night to think about it. Sure enough, next morning we had ten new names although a few were a bit bizarre. What I learned is what it takes to stretch the mind so that a 'brainspark' turns into new and creative solutions. The first ten are easy—the eleventh requires effort. The first round is painless, the second is a challenge and the third demands expansion into new territory. That's how we get to thirty-three—$(10 + 1) \times 3$!

An easy way to understand the reasoning behind the 'rule of 33' is to think of it as a road trip to a destination where you've never been before. The first one-third of your trip will be very comfortable—after all, it is territory you already know—your driveway, your neighborhood and your city. The second one-third may not be quite as familiar but it will likely not represent any unusual challenge—perhaps it is across your own State where you have traveled before. It is the last one-third, to the place where you haven't ever been before, the uncharted territory that represents the unknown, that presents the challenge. This road can be the most exciting part of the trip—so don't stop until you get there. And don't stop brainsparking until you get to the place you've not explored yet.

Keep in mind that creativity is a one-on-one sport and innovation is a team sport. Allow your team members to come up with ideas, but remember that it takes the entire team to implement them.

I have gotten to know Jeff a little better over the past couple of months and he has shared that he is just getting to know the Project Management world. He is doing a great job because he keeps alluding to excellent practices that really great PMs make use of all the time. This Chapter is a perfect example.

How many meetings have you participated (particularly if it was not your meeting but you needed to be, or were required to be there) where one highly verbal person has dominated the discussion for over an hour and you are still no closer to a resolution? We love those meetings, right? No, of course none of us do. So, how do you overcome the dominant control person rambling on forever, without offending them, and still ending up with buy-in from the whole team? Jeff's 33 ideas is one way since it forces movement beyond one person's thought.

Another approach we have found amazingly effective is the "Five Fives". This comes out of the Scrum community and is a great 'speed to solution' technique that anyone can use immediately and with great results. Here is how it goes;

1. Give everyone a blank sheet of paper and a pad of small (3" x 3") Post It notes.
2. Write the question or problem on the white board
3. Instruct every person in the room (it does not matter how many you have but it gets unwieldy when you move past 9 or 10 participants) to write one solution or idea per Post It note and put it on their paper. Everyone should try to come up with 5 ideas.
4. Set a timer for 5 minutes.
5. At the end of 5 minutes everyone passes their paper to the right and receives the paper from the person to their left.

6. The next 5 minutes is still spent quietly reviewing the ideas from another person. This will cause you to expand what is written on a Post It note or will spark a fresh idea.

7. Repeat the hand off and review another one or two times.

8. Take a break and have the facilitator group all the ideas (Post It notes) into circles on the white board with a title for each group. Of course there are usually one or two stand-alone ideas that get their own circle.

9. Bring the group back together and then dot vote on the best ideas. This means everyone gets a few sticky dots they can place in the circle of the ideas they think are best. (if there are 10 groups/circles you should give everyone 3 or 4 dots)

10. Once everyone has voted put another color circle around the highest 4 or 5 vote totals and then vote again but this time each person gets 2 dots to vote with.

This narrows the discussion down to the one or two best ideas that the group has agreed on and you are only a half hour into the meeting. You can now discuss approaches to the two best ideas without wasting time on ideas or solutions that only one person thought had merit.

If you are interested in additional ideas the book "Agile Retrospectives: Making Good Teams Great" by Esther Derby and Diana Larson, is a great resource.

You want to get to a place of action. Facilitate meetings that take you there and you will find that you have avoided many mind numbing monologues. Your team will thank you for it. You will thank you for it.

House On Wheels

Get Outside Your Comfort Zone to Find Answers

On a dreary day in November, I found myself reading the Sunday newspaper when I came across a full-page, full-color advertisement for the Recreational Vehicle Show coming to my hometown of Pittsburgh. Please don't be offended, but I tease people who dream of retiring and 'seeing the country' in an R.V. by asking them why in the world they would want to carry their houses on their backs. Just not my dream!

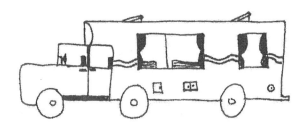

My advertising background made me more interested in the obvious expense this show went to for this advertisement. I turned the newspaper towards my wife who was sitting opposite me on the sofa.

"Look at this," I explained. "What a waste of advertising!"

I did not even get the newspaper turned back around before my wife retorted, "Excuse me?"

"What?" I asked.

"Oh, Mr. Creativity himself. Isn't it you that tells people to get outside of their comfort zones and try things a little different?" she challenged.

I just nodded my head and she ordered, "GO!"

"Go where?" I asked.

"Go to the R.V. show"

"I am NOT going to the R.V. show!" I declared.

When I was at the R.V. show...I was immediately enraptured by the 'toys' I found there! I was so impressed that the following summer, I rented a thirty-two foot R.V. in Calgary, Alberta and took my family on a ten-day adventure through the Canadian Rockies. It was the most incredible trip of our lives. All because I forced myself—OK! I was forced—to go to the R.V. show!

Many of the answers to the challenges we face in our lives do not lie within the 'four walls' of our lives. We need to constantly and consciously force ourselves to do some things that are very uncomfortable to be more creative.

I like this Chapter because Jeff is heeding his own advice here. Go do something that is completely outside your normal path to shake up your world view and expand your broader understanding of how things are or how they work.

From a project management point of view, my advice here is to choose to do something outside your comfort zone. If you have never gone jumped out of a plane - go do it. If you have never gone white water rafting—hit the road and make it happen. If you have never programmed a computer—join a programmers meet-up group (easy to find in almost any city in America). There are even innovation groups that meet to make things and everyone learns from everyone else as they concentrate on a project. The one in Grand Rapids is called GR Makers. It is 8,500 square feet of space with 3D printers and saws and other machines as well as materials to make things. A day pass is $8 and it will stretch your mind, particularly if you go when the geeks are meeting to build things. It also sounds like a great break-out event for a project team to help build unity and relationships. Go make something fun as a team.

You could also go to a sporting show (if you have never hunted, for example), or the RV show, or rent a motor home. Break your patterns and stay fresh. Ideas will flow as a result.

A Modern Fairy Tale

See the World Through Your Clients' Eyes and Change Your Perspective

Allow me to relate a modern fairy tale. It takes place in a land with a very deep and fast flowing river running right through the middle. No one is able to cross the river by themselves without drowning. On one side of the river, we find Miss A. On the other side of the river, Mr. B. Now, over time Miss A and Mr. B have developed quite a relationship by just talking across the river. It occurs to them that they are deeply in love. But, the river poses quite an obstacle. One day, Miss A turns to Mr. B and, professing her love, she asks him to stay put

while she walks down the levee to try to find a way across. Not far away, Miss A comes upon Mr. C. who has a boat. Passionate about getting across the river, she explains her dilemma to Mr. C and asks him to ferry her so that she can be with her true love.

Mr. C agrees to take Miss A across the river—if she will kiss him. Miss A is taken aback and refuses to kiss Mr. C because of her love for Mr. B. Mr. C simply restates his 'price', only to be rejected once more. Distraught, Miss A trudges further along the riverbank. Soon she encounters Mr. D! Mr. D is sitting in a rocking chair minding his own business when Miss A approaches. She explains the whole situation and she begs for Mr. D's assistance. Mr. D refuses! He explains, in no uncertain terms, that he doesn't want to get involved. He feels that this is none of his business and he asks Miss A to leave him alone.

Feeling defeated, Miss A decides to exercise her only viable option as she treks back to Mr. C and acquiesces to his demands. True to his word, Mr. C takes Miss A across the river in his boat. Miss A makes her way along the other side of the river, soon to be in the arms of her true love.

As she approaches Mr. B, he calls out to her, asking her to explain how she got there. Miss A tells him the whole sordid story leaving no stone unturned. After listening to all of this and without hesitation, Mr. B turns to Miss A and informs her that he doesn't want her anymore. He explains that his standards are very clear and, since she kissed Mr. C, he could no longer accept her!

Confused and forlorn, Miss A trudges along the riverbank without any idea of what to do. Suddenly she comes across Mr. E! Mr. E is on a horse—a white horse— and he is dressed in white. After Miss A explains the whole situation, Mr. E only takes a second to consider his options. He explains to Miss A that he doesn't care about her past and that he loves her just the way she is. He invites her to join him on his horse as they ride off into the sunset together. She does! They do! End of story.

After you have put your tissues away, if I were to ask you to rate our five characters according to how much you respect them, how do you think your list would look? Perhaps you would put Miss A at the top because of her stamina, her perseverance or her tenacity. Perhaps she would be at the bottom of your list because she compromised herself? Did you respect Mr. B the most because he was principled? Or, perhaps the least because he was inflexible? Maybe Mr. C would top your list because he had a price and stuck to it, or he could be at the bottom because he was obviously an opportunist. Did you respect Mr. D because of his ability to stay uninvolved? Or perhaps you didn't like the fact that he would not help a damsel in distress! Finally, maybe you put Mr. E at the top of your column; the knight in shining armor, able to accept our heroine no matter what her past. Or is Mr. E really the opportunist in this story?

The point is that these are all right. The word that should come to mind is *perspective*. The ability to understand that in any given situation, someone else may have a totally different perspective of the same information. Recognize that world class marketers always take this into account. They see the world through their market's eyes, allowing them to see the way their market buys. The next time you prepare for a stakeholder meeting, or prep for your weekly status update session, or email a valued vendor who is critical to your project's success, stop and consider their perspective. What is important to them, not you? It will change the discussion and increase value.

I enjoyed this story when Jeff presented the live version of it. It caused people in the room, including me, to think. We had to twist the assumptions around in our heads and look at the other perspectives that might be operating in addition to their own personal bias or understanding.

We have trained this "walk in the other person's shoes" mindset for decades using Wilson Learning's Social Styles. This system gives broad buckets for identifying how people are most comfortable in social interactions and how you can 'flex' into their comfort zone to more effectively communicate with them. Of course DiSC, Meyer-Briggs and others do a similar breakdown. A simple and quick one is Strength Finders from the Gallop organization. You buy the book and it gives you a link to take a short survey that then ranks your highest five strengths and some information about those strengths. We strongly recommend that you invest in understanding yourself better and those you are interacting with by utilizing some of these excellent tools. It will help you understand other people's perspectives.

One caution—when I took the Strength Finders questionnaire I was surprised that they immediately offered me a full refund upon completion. The reason given was that 'for the first time in the history of the Gallop organization the survey came up with "no discernible strengths found!".

OK, that did not happen. But I did fill out the questionnaire and was surprised at how accurate it was. Take your team through this exercise and use it as a discussion starter to spark positive interactions with each other as a team. Then try and ID some of the strengths your Stakeholders have and how those strengths might inform how you engage and communicate with them.

What This Means To You Is...

The Real Scoop on Benefits Versus Features in Your Business

In my former capacity as a sales and marketing consultant, I often liked to travel with some outside representatives of any company with which I was about to work. It was an eye-opening experience when you have no vested interest in the outcome of the call and you can truly sit back and listen to the exchange. Oh sure, I wanted them to succeed, but I was interested more in the reaction of their prospects.

I once spent the day with a woman from a large promotional products company on the west coast. Rhonda was a little nervous as she knew that this experience might be put under a microscope when the entire company convened the next day for training. Yet, the owner of the firm had assured me that Rhonda was the most professional and successful representative that they had working in the field. I tried to assuage her fears by guaranteeing that I was not there to be a critic, but rather to observe.

Now, Rhonda had spent an enormous amount of time and energy in preparing a power point presentation to WOW potential clients. I was immediately impressed at how prepared she was going into our first meeting of the day with a committee who was to decide about a new safety program for their factory. Rhonda was professional to a tee and her ability to relate to all of the personalities in the room was envious.

As the slide show began, I could feel the anticipation in the room because this group had obviously not been treated to this level of professionalism in the past. The first slide showed a graphic of Rhonda's company logo. Cascading into the frame was a large bullet point, "Since 1892". She explained that her firm, ABC Company (the names have been changed to protect the innocent!), had been in business since 1892. The next bullet to appear simply read, "Largest" and she offered that ABC Company was the largest distributor of its kind on the west coast. As the third bullet appeared, I looked around the room to looks of various levels of interest. One gentleman had begun doodling on his notepad and a woman opposite me was giving one of those continuous nods of agreement.

When Rhonda finished fifteen minutes later, there were some courteous questions and we were dismissed. As we approached her car, Rhonda looked at me and asked what she had done wrong. She said that she knew that she didn't get the account because she had not "clicked" with the committee. I was stumped, but I knew that she had not held their interest.

As we drove to the next presentation, it hit me. I always contend that your clients only listen to one radio station around the world—WIIfm (What's In It For Me!). They don't care that you have been in business for 1000 years and that you are the best in the world. They want to know how that translates to a benefit for them. I offered a solution to Rhonda. "What if—in this next call—you give the exact same presentation, but *every* time you give one of your bulleted points, you offered two benefits to the group?"

After considering this challenge, Rhonda agreed but interrogated me further as to how she could do that. I explained that there is a very simple formula to ensure that one always keeps the benefits in mind. Every time you offer a response—a feature—follow it up with some form of the words, "what this means to you is…". Then, when you finish this, you repeat, "what this also means to you is…". Rhonda agreed to try it.

The next meeting was with only two people looking for the perfect giveaways for an upcoming company-wide picnic. The presentation began. The first bullet appeared and Rhonda started her monologue.

"We have been in business since 1892. What this means to you is that you will be working with a well-established company—not a fly-by-night. What this also means is that, because we have more experience in promotional advertising than any other company in the area, we have more resources to offer our clients." Not bad! Not bad!

The next bullet appeared. *"Largest"*. Rhonda piped in, "We are the largest distributor of our kind on the west coast so we are able to pass on volume discounts to you, saving you money. This also allows you peace of mind in knowing that there is always someone in our office who can help you, even if I am out on the road." *Touché!*

Now, I don't want to brag or anything, but Rhonda got the order on the spot. Her clients loved her presentation which she masterfully had altered with only the words she used.

My challenge to you is to look at what you do for a living. Look at your business. Ask yourself whether or not you are offering benefits at *every* opportunity you can. When you introduce yourself to someone do you simply tell them what you do (features) or do you tell them what you can do for them (benefits)? When you exhibit at a trade show, does the sign in the back of your booth boast your company name (features) or what your company can do for someone who is interested (benefits).

By the way, Rhonda called me the other day to ask my advice on something else. She asked for advice and continued, "What offering this advice means to you is...."!

"Lord Ronald said nothing; he flung himself from the room, flung himself upon his horse and rode madly off in all directions."

> Canadian humorist *Stephen Leacock*
> in his story *Gertrude the Governess*

The advice Jeff gave Rhonda applies to many areas within the project management universe. When you are given the Project Charter (I should probably say "if" you are given the project charter since many projects begin with the intent or vision assumed and not spelled out in a clear charter document) you need to begin asking the WIIFM questions;

- What is the value or benefit to the entire organization for the successful completion of this project?
- What Strategic initiative will this project fulfill upon completion?
- How will my division or functional unit benefit?
- What is the direct benefit to each team member for participating on this project team?
- What is in it for me (too)

If you can clearly articulate the answers to these questions then the other aspects of running the project will fall into place with more clarity. Do not assume. If the project was initiated with assumptions it is up to you to demand clarity and if it is not forthcoming then create it as best you can. This is not a small thing. This is *the* thing. It helps maintain focus on the benefits and not the features or individual requirements. The features and requirements are there to fulfill a purpose. Identify that purpose and stay focused on it. In the military, this is called the 'commander's intent': the short description of why the team is working to complete this particular project.

Simon Sinek outlines the importance of this very well in his book, "Start with Why". On page 67 he encourages us to form each values statement as a verb; "For values or guiding principles to be truly effective they have to be verbs. It's not 'integrity', it's 'always do the right thing.' It's not 'innovation,' it's 'look at the problem from another angle.' Articulating our values as verbs gives us a clear idea … we have a clear idea of how to act in any situation." The same clarity is needed for each "why" statement for each party or organizational unit. It is the job of the PM to understand the "why" and orient her team to the delivery of it.

In the Unified Vision Framework we call this effort Cascading the VSPT. We articulated the VSPT (Vision, Strategy, People and Tasks) in an earlier chapter. It is amazingly effective at establishing and maintaining team buy-in. Also, the effective delivery of this mindset and activity will cause your communications, and ultimately your project, to succeed beyond your highest expectations. In other words, you will not fling yourself on your project horse and madly ride off in all directions.

Why Different Can Be Good

Re-Creating the Category in Which You Currently Compete

If you are feeling the heat of new competition lately, you are probably doing something right.

A couple of days ago, I was surveying the shelves of my local pharmacy. A summer cold had gotten hold of me While browsing through all of the latest cold medicines, one caught my attention; "Thera Flu" from Sandoz Pharmaceuticals.

This is not an endorsement for the product, but the name Thera Flu versus all of the others which had "cold" in their name was the attraction. As a matter of fact, upon closer scrutiny, I realized that Thera Flu has the exact same ingredients as most of the other cold remedies. But it's not a cold remedy. It's a flu remedy. In my mind, that put Thera Flu all by itself in a whole new category. This is marketing at a different level.

It occurs to me that successful businesses attract competitors the way sugar draws ants. The more you grow, the more others are thinking about how they can steal away the markets you have built.

One way to stay a step ahead: Change the rules in the middle of the game. That's obviously what Sandoz Pharmaceuticals has done. I can only guess that when me-too competitors started to elbow their way into the long established category of cold remedy medicines, Sandoz figured it may be time to shift gears and create a whole new category. That got them out of the "ours is better than theirs" trap.

I began looking for other companies who have re-created their category. I found a financial services company that positioned itself as the leader in healthcare equipment leasing—even though its "healthcare" leases worked just like any other lease. They were the first in this new category.

What about the first printing firm who declared themselves a "quick printer"? Other printers probably had the same capabilities, but customers in a hurry will go to the quick printer first.

As I became more aware of this marketing ploy, I began to understand that when creative marketers can't continue to create new categories, they still try to change the rules. They simply turn their weaknesses into strengths and their competitors' strengths into weaknesses.

Accentuate your negatives and turn them into positives. If you succeed, the competitor's marketing of your negatives will actually reinforce *your* message. I remember Warner-Lambert marketing Listerine as "the taste you hate twice a day." A perfect example. What about Smuckers— hardly an appetizing name—who boasted, "With a name like Smuckers, it has to be good."?

If this doesn't apply to you, then look at **turning your competitor's strengths into weaknesses**. When a competitor dominates the market because of a unique competency—for example, because it has a patented process—it may think it has a lock on the market. The best example of this? How about *"7-Up—The*

Un-Cola"? These are opportunities waiting to present themselves to you.

Customers hate feeling beholden to a single supplier—no matter how well that supplier treats them. And they may go to surprising lengths to be sure they have other options. I recently worked with a telecommunications company which was researching a new technology that could compete against satellites to carry TV programming. But the technology still needed a lot of expensive research and development. To my surprise, I found that several of the major networks had pitched in to help. Even though they were happy with what they were using, they wanted other options—just in case.

No other book which focused on this specific marketing strategy is better than the 2005 publication, *Blue Ocean Strategy: How to Create Uncontested Market Space and Make Competition Irrelevant* by W. Chan Kim and Renee Mauborgne. A blue ocean strategy is the simultaneous pursuit of differentiation and low cost to open up a new market space and create new demand. One of the examples the authors illustrated was Cirque Du Soleil. The founders of Cirque simply asked themselves, "what if we could deliver a circus without any animals?" That took them into a whole new market where they could charge hundreds of dollars for a ticket versus the tens-of-dollars that the traditional circuses were charging.

What small thing could you do to re-position yourself in your world that could change the way you do business?

"If you are not guided by Vision You Will Be Driven By Circumstance"

The PMO Brothers in "The Nehemiah Effect: Ancient Wisdom From the World's First Agile Projects"

How are Project Managers perceived in your organization? Transactional? Task level delivery people? Management overhead? Strategic partners?

Most, unfortunately, are not seen as strategic even if perceived as valuable at the task level. This is also why many reports show that 30% of all Program or Project Management Offices will be shut down within the next 18 months. That is the current failure rate for these offices. Why? They are set up with the expectation that they will normalize tools, processes and practices across the enterprise and, by focused reporting, manage the competing interests wrangling over resource allocation. When the corporate anti-bodies rise up in resistance and the tactics level operational improvements have not occurred, senior management pulls the plug.

Had they begun the process with a strategic intention and linked the office and all projects to the overarching Purpose, Mission and Vision of the organization, the value would be seen because it would be perceived through a different lens.

Here is a street level example. In the late 1990's, I was brought in as the external project lead on a Customer Relationship Management (CRM) system for a multi-billion dollar manufacturing company. It was an end-to-end CRM system from the call center first contact points down to how corrective action was initiated and completed on the plant floor. The project was in flames and there was a high risk that senior management was going to shutter the project and consider it failed.

We had two weeks until the go/no go meeting with the executives. We were housed in an old run down building on the campus and there was a large, unoccupied room adjacent to our team area. We commandeered it for a team war room. On one end we posted the Company Vision statement from the website in large type on an 11x17 page. Below that we posted the 11 strategic initiatives in focus for that year. We highlighted the one that lined up most appropriately with our CRM project and put a piece of yarn between the Vision and the Strategic initiative. The following week we found two quotes from the CEO and President of the North American Division in the Wall Street Journal and another in Business Weekly related to the importance of Customer Service, so we stretched yarn leading back to the Strategic Initiative.

We then printed out and taped to the wall the five page Project Charter (which we created during the two weeks as well) and put yarn from the Strategic Initiative to the Charter and a high-level Milestone Chart.

Lastly, we took a desk-top blank calendar and filled it out with the Milestones and critical cross-dependent activities needed to deliver the project.

We used the room instead of power point to walk the Executives through the project's current status and future deliverables. When the meeting ended one of the Executives turned to another and stated, "This is the best organized project in the history of the Company!"

That was not an accurate assessment due to the underlying mess that still had to be worked through but it did reflect the intention of the reorganization and how the team was going to focus to deliver. It also provided us favor and grace to continue with the project.

So how does this work together with Jeff's example where a re-packaged medication sold better with a different name?

You can re-package a project using the language of leadership (Vision and Strategies being utilized for delivering it). When you do, you may find the exact same facts can find a more receptive audience.

We are not suggesting you misrepresent anything. We certainly did not candy coat any of the current facts. Just realize that 'different can be good,' particularly when the difference is pointing at the reason everyone is there.

The Sunshine State

Understanding the Four Market Sectors to Whom We Must Appeal

I recently read an article in a magazine by an author whom I admire. He began by superficially describing his surroundings on the beautiful, tropical island of Maui and I immediately lost all respect for him. So, I am pondering whether or not to let you know that I am sitting in the Florida Keys as the Northeast endures another mid-winter northerner.

You see, the only reasons I went to Florida Keys Tourism Board has taught me a very valuable marketing lesson that I must share with you. You see, the only reason I have come to Florida in the recent past was to visit my parents who lived here six months of the year or because work brings me here. I would never *choose* to come here for pleasure's sake...until now. My impression is that it is crowded, nobody knows how to drive and the weather is unpredictable. Why go to Florida?

Believe it or not, it was a 60 second commercial I saw on television about four months ago while sitting in my living room watching my favorite football team get pummeled by some other team that convinced me that marketing works. It was a spoof of the stereotype I had of the Sunshine State. The camera shot was from behind a car, obviously in Miami Beach. All you could see were two hands on the steering wheel and the car gliding along a 4 lane road (down the center line) at about 15MPH. Then they cut to Daytona Beach where they showed a teenager, sitting atop a van on the beach toasting the camera with a beer in her hand as she simultaneously turned away to vomit over the side. The caption? (paraphrasing...) *"The Florida Keys...Unlike What You Would Expect in the Rest of the State."* It was funny and it caught my attention and ultimately my pocketbook.

During that same football game, the Florida Keys Tourism Board had another, much shorter advertisement. It showed a man sitting in a hole he had dug on the beach as if he was building sand castles. His wife and children played in the surf as he first waved at them then turned his attention to his building. The camera pans behind him and now displays a laptop and telephone in the hole. The caption? *"Nobody Needs To Know You're Still Open For Business...The Florida Keys."*

It doesn't sound like a real marketing coup, but I realized what the tourism board had done. Something that is what we call 'the new age of marketing'. No longer can we look at a one-size-fits-all marketing approach in our businesses. As these ads showed me, we must consider that there are 4 very distinct markets out there. If your advertising, your business' physical environment, your every marketing effort, does not appeal to every one of these styles—either individually or as a group—you are losing out on potential customers.

I have developed nicknames for the four groups of potential clients. You can name them what you like! (Please don't write letters about gender, equality etc. None of these are better than the others. We need all four types to be successful in any business.)

Factoid Fred

Fred wants just the facts. This potential customer simply wants to know the benefit of doing business with you or of using your product or service. They can't be bothered with all of the details. Remember the man building sand castles? This appeals to Factoid Fred because he can get away with his family and still be in touch when he needs to be. He makes quick decisions based on the benefits he perceives that you offer. Fred thrives on a challenge or problem-solving quest. When we market to Fred we must keep it short and to the point. Don't get cutesy and don't waste his time with humorous anecdotes.

Entertain-Me Edna

Edna is the prospect to whom most sales organizations appeal. She likes FUN anyway you can package it. The spoof of the Florida stereotype appeals to all of your Entertain-Me Ednas because it of its lighthearted approach. Like our Factoid Freds, don't bother Edna with details... not because they can't be bothered, but because they are less organized and more likely to forget. Give Edna a cute 800 number that spells out something. Let them know you will take care of the details. Act like their friend and prove to Ednas that, by using the solution you offer, they will be part of the in-crowd. Impress Edna with testimonials.

Even Steven

Even Steven likes to know that everything will go smoothly in using what you are offering. They are very much team players in their work environment and translate 'team' to mean family. When marketing to Steven, we must consider their family values and that it is vital to show them why our solution will help the team/organization. Stevens require more details than the first two and they require an upfront plan if things should go wrong. Steven loves 1-800-HELP lines that are available 24 hours or a money-back guarantee. Even Steven is still a people person so don't get too technical, but ensure him that things will go *evenly*.

Detail Doris

This is the sector of the population that most people ignore. Detail Doris needs just that—DETAILS. Like our Factoid Freds, they are no-bull, get-down-to-business types. But unlike Fred, they require information overload. One of the most effective means of targeting this group was the final advertisement I observed on that cold November day in my living room. The entire commercial—and remember, this is for the beauty of the tropical Florida Keys—simply showed a spreadsheet divided in two. On one side are the *Pros* of taking a vacation to the Florida Keys and on the other, the *Cons* of taking the trip. The camera pulls back to show a woman in her office with her walls papered in graphs, charts and spreadsheets, all relating to the possibility of indulging in a Florida Keys vacation. The voice over? "All the *facts* point towards the Florida Keys for your next family vacation." This hits at the very persona of Detail Doris.

In a more sophisticated, marketing world, we look at market segmentation from either a demographic or psychographic perspective. Maybe this approach is enough to truly allow you to understand your prospects and your customers! Present this concept to your team and tell them to categorize people in their minds as they decide how to approach them with an opportunity. Then brainspark ideas of how to do this with the four different behavioral styles. Once you have this and it is specific to your business, it will make it much easier for them to do what they do!

Here again we can use Jeff's approach to freshen up how we view our communications to Customers or Stakeholders. It might be fun for your team to take a few minutes as an exercise to draw avatars of Fred, Edna, Steven and Doris. Use the big flip chart Post It notes and create one for each figure. At the bottom write the approach that best suites this personality type; Quick facts, Stories, Team room Visible flow to demonstrate movement and unity, and Details. Put the names of all the relevant Customers and Stakeholders on 2"x2" PostIt notes and then have a discussion as to which picture each named sticky note should be placed. It will help the entire team understand how these diverse and important people receive and process information differently. This will give you great information as a team to form a cogent and effective communications plan.

Make it fun but realize this type of understanding will accelerate success for you project so also make it real.

Are Your Bagels Hot?

How to Appeal to All of the Senses of Your Customers

The other morning I was sitting in my local bagel shop enjoying my coffee, bagel and newspaper. I am not sure what prompted me to look up, but the first thing that struck me was that this establishment obviously did a booming morning business. People stood in line 15 deep and didn't seem to mind the wait. As I was pondering the idea of having people stand in line for what I have to offer, another curiosity struck me. It had nothing to do with the customers or even the counter personnel. It was the bagel maker who got my attention.

I watched as he carefully manipulated a tray of steaming hot bagels into the metal bins with appropriate labeling according to the flavor. He then proceeded to add a little sign—bright red with white letters—to those bins to which he had just contributed. The sign? "HOT". Nothing extraordinary in and of itself, but the reaction was immediate. The very next patron to order, demanded some of the 'hot' bagels. And so did the next. And the next. Soon the bagel maker re-appeared with another tray and followed the same routine with another flavor. And guess what? The same results. The customers switched their "flavor-of-the-minute" and their attention to the new bin labeled "HOT".

This little ritual went on for the next forty-five minutes and I felt like I had discovered the marketing idea of the century. I got up the nerve during a lull in the action (there was a few minutes when there were no 'hot' bagels available) and I approached the young lady donning the manager nametag. When I inquired as to this phenomenon, she threw back her head and laughed. "You caught us! You uncovered our entire marketing strategy."

My new marketing guru explained to me that the powers-that-be in her company had always subscribed to the idea that to market, one must appeal to as many senses of the customer, or prospective customer, as possible. "Sense of smell and taste were taken care of in this environment," she explained. "But bagels are bagels and they all pretty much look the same." She went on to detail how they had discovered the "HOT" strategy completely by mistake. Originally, they had put the signs on to warn store personnel of the impending danger in handling steaming hot bagels. What they discovered was a huge increase in demand, by their customers, on any particular flavor that was adorned with the little sign. She finished rather defensively by explaining that they did not manipulate their customers, but simply appealed to another sense—sight. I suddenly understood the reason why the shop did not seem to anticipate daily consumption and bake bagels in advance of the rush.

The obvious lesson I took from this is that we must figure out ways to appeal to all of our customer's senses. Some have it easier than others. I believe that, someone who works in the food arena for example, has a great 'one-up' on the banker, the insurance broker or the accountant. The 'outside-the-lines' marketing idea that occurred to me was this: How can I entice my customers with the "hot" item or service of the moment? I can't use a little red sign, but I could give the same impression.

One florist, with whom we have consulted, imports Holland tulips during months in which her market typically can't find tulips—hot item! A local restaurateur who promotes a certain type of snapper served a certain kind of way "upon availability" tells me that it is his most popular dish. By the way, I frequent that restaurant and have never been told the snapper is *not* available—hot item!

The possibilities seem endless. Take a look at your product, your service or even yourself and ask yourself, "Do my customers perceive my '*bagels*' as being HOT???"

This Chapter highlights the impact and positive effect of utilizing all of the senses in sales and marketing, but it's also vital to project management.

Most project managers do not see themselves in a 'sales' role. They are the delivery people who drive tasks to successful completion within a planned framework. However, PMs ignore the truth this chapter brings to their own peril.

The most successful projects I have ever been on (this is Ted) have used all of the senses in managing the flow of the project. For example, in the late 90s my brother Andrew and I were working together on a telecom project, DNA Finland, in Helsinki Finland as part of the edgecom (Ericsson's consulting group at that time) team. One of the other consultant teams working with us was from Cap Gemini. They had constructed what they called "The Big Brown Monster" in one of the conference rooms. This was the overall project chart on a piece of 4 foot wide craft paper strung out along one of the walls. It had multiple swim lanes and milestones and dates and it filled the entire wall. This is where the weekly status meetings were held and everyone could see all of the project parts as they moved toward milestones and ultimate completion. It worked well.

Today we see this in the Agile environments like Scrum. You have a Kanban board in the team room that holds all of the Product Backlog items (the work breakdown structure of Agile for you more traditional PMs), as well as the work being done in the current Sprint of two to four weeks and what each team member is working on and has completed today and during the Sprint. This adds 'sight' as a sense that is engaged in the PM process.

Agile engages the sense of 'touch' by having each team member move their own work items (called User Stories or Tasks) from "Doing" to "Done" on the Kanban board. A physical movement that adds completion and finality to the task and allows discussions around items that are stalled or blocked.

The sense of 'hearing' is drawn in for every team member during the Daily Stand-up meeting where everyone reports what was done, what is blocked and what they will be doing. This is the auditory connection for everyone.

'Taste' is not a part of the experience yet, but perhaps you could track down Jeff's bagel joint and surprise your team with some "Hot Bagels" to round out the sensory chorus.

Take away? Look for ways within your current project flow (be it traditional, waterfall or agile) to increase the utilization of all the team members senses and watch productivity and creativity increase. It happens every time.

Does Customer Service Have Anything to do with Marketing?

Word of Mouth tells Others About YOU!

GREAT customer experience has everything to do with marketing! I tell audiences around the world that customer experiences are something you offer whether or not you are a company or an individual. It doesn't matter if you are 'serving' an internal or an external customer you have an amazing opportunity to make your mark!

Consider this customer service story. I walked into Nordstrom in the Dallas Galleria intent on purchasing a pair of running shoes I knew they carried. After being approached by a friendly (but not overly-friendly) salesperson named James, he asked me a series of questions about my desire for that particular shoe. By analyzing my answers, James convinced me that another shoe was far more appropriate for the multi-use needs that I had. He went to get me the shoes to try on.

James returned with nothing in his hands and a disappointed look in his eyes. He informed me that he was out of stock but that he could order them and have them delivered to me. Quite honestly, I didn't want the shoes that badly. I am a 'instant gratification" kind of guy and if I couldn't have them now, I could find them back home.

James persisted. "Mr. Tobe, are you going to be in the Mall for awhile?" I hesitated but informed him that I planned on having lunch before I left. He replied, "Let me try to find the shoes. Come back when you are finished eating."

I agreed and left thinking that this was odd. There was only one Nordstrom store in Dallas at the time, so how could he produce my shoes in the next forty-five minutes?

When I returned, James was beaming. He had the shoes! As I tried them on, I noticed a price tag on the box from an athletic shoe store also found in the mall; a competitor! James had gone to the other store, purchased the shoes and had them ready for me. Not only that but, the price on the tag was two dollars more than the price James was quoting me. When I inquired as to why he had done this, he replied, "Mr. Tobe, it is worth the effort and the extra two dollars to make sure you come back to us next time you are in Dallas"

Needless to say, I had no choice but to buy the shoes right then and there. More importantly, I have now shared this example with 1000's of people in my workshops and keynotes. And now I am sharing it with thousands of you!

When you make a great impression, people talk about you. There are all kinds of studies that basically show that if you do something right people will tell many people about their experience. Do something wrong and they will tell many MORE. We constantly have to keep considering how our actions are going to have repercussions. Like the stone thrown into the smooth waters of the pond—it's all about the ripple!

Look for opportunities to develop a personal and professional friendship. Friends will not only enhance business, but they can bring balance to the pressures of work. This is just the tip of the iceberg. If you constantly keep word-of-mouth marketing at the top of your mind and if you consistently promote this to your team, you can't help but offer better service and a better buying experience. Someone once said that it is not the problems in business that can kill you—it's what you do OR don't do about them!

"Let Another Man Speak Your Praise"

Ancient Proverb

Having a third party speak well of you has always been the most powerful endorsement you could receive. Stories like the action taken by the Nordstrom clerk are potent because they are rare and because customer service of this type is opposite to the experience many people encounter at most businesses. We do not even need to bring up examples. We have all experienced the dark side.

Nordstrom actually has a policy that allows any employee to spend up to a certain level on anything they choose if they believe it will delight the customer and generate this type of response. This is also rare and so not applicable to project management.

So why is it still in the book? First, because it reflects an attitude of service and that will always have a positive impact on your project. Service toward your team and also your customer or stakeholder in areas that have nothing to do with the project deliverables will be remembered long after the project has wrapped up and the lessons learned loaded into the company knowledge base file. IT is the currency of positive relationship that brings benefits over and over in the same way that Jeff is still talking about the clerk years later.

Second, you can facilitate third party endorsement of your project, with a little effort, that will reap huge dividends. A story here will help. We were working on a project for a large multi-national company, and one of the team members had made the decision to no longer use a vendor to develop a piece of software due to non-performance and a lack of confidence that the vendor could ever deliver what was needed. That was fine. The issue was that the vendor team was led by a former college football teammate and roommate of the CEO. This created some noise and discomfort for our team.

The team had turned the project around and found a unique way to solve the technical and organizational issues and had begun to successfully roll out the software, but the rumble of the noise continued.

We had the team create an article about the successful project and then pitched the article to seven different publications; The Wall Street Journal, Crains Business, etc. The article was turned down by everyone except CIO Magazine and they ran it (almost with any changes) as a feature article. When it was published we bought enough copies to place one on every chair in the executive suite (opened to the page with the positive article about our project).

Having another person sing our praise removed the noise and we were able to use the article in advancing the success of the roll out as well.

Third party endorsements are indeed powerful. There are trade journals, local business papers, business sections to the local paper, tech writers who freelance, or even the weekly papers that get distributed to every home in your area that are looking to find stories, content to fill their columns. If you write a draft article and send it along to these potential outlets you will be surprised how many times you can get something published.

Does it take time and effort? Yes. Is it worth the time and effort to obtain a powerful communications tool for your project or team? You be the judge. For us the answer has been a resounding yes.

Experience Customer Service

It's Gone Beyond Customer Service

Let's talk about customer service! It just has not been discussed, dissected and examined enough over the last few years. (Hint of sarcasm there!) In visiting my local on-line bookstore, I realized that there are more books written on customer service than any other business topic today. The sad part is that I also realized that I have read many of them.

Don't get me wrong. There's probably not a more important topic than the 'service' we offer our customers, but I think things have changed. Those organizations that recognize the next wave in customer service will be the ones who ultimately 'serve' their market better than any others. Those organizations that consider this will gain the competitive "edge". When you think of organizations the likes of Nordstrom, Saturn, and Starbuck's, we automatically think that customer service is the one thing that separates them from the pack. This is not entirely true.

Imagine for a moment that I have a handful of coffee beans in my palm. I take those beans to my local MacDonald's and they make me a coffee for about a dollar. Now, take those same beans (alright, maybe you can argue that they are a better quality bean, but that's inconsequential in this illustration) over to this relatively-new phenomenon called Starbuck's, and they make me a cup of coffee and charge about three dollars. Is the service really any different at Starbuck's vs. MacDonald's? As a matter of fact, the senior citizens at my MacDonald's are the friendliest, most accommodating people I know. No, it's gone beyond customer service.

Continuing on with our handful of coffee beans...

A few years ago, I had the fortuitous opportunity to spend a few days of R&R on the island of Bali in the South Pacific. Add to that the splendor of the Four Season's Resort—a Five Star hotel—recently rated as one of the top five resorts in the ENTIRE world. Our private, thatched roof, dining room—open on three sides to the beach and

the Pacific—was the setting for breakfast each morning. Remember our coffee beans? A cup of coffee at the Four Season's Hotel cost something in the neighborhood of seven dollars. AND WE PAID IT! Why?

You see, it wasn't the service, although I have NEVER had service as personalized and attentive as we did at this resort. But breakfast, once delivered to our villa, was still just a meal! No, it was THE EXPERIENCE. People are more than willing to pay for the experience if it is unique, personalized and responsive. When was the last time you considered the experience that your client—internal or external—has with you each time they interact with you? From the first moment they make contact with you until the moment they are finished with you. It's no longer about customer service but rather, it's about the experience.

I tell retailers all of the time to walk into their place of business tomorrow. What is the first thing you see? What is the first thing you smell? What is the first thing you hear? This all affects the experience their customers have with them. Do you entertain team members in your office? When they walk in, you can ask these same questions. You have been going there for years and maybe you are used to the musty carpet smell! Get Learn to alleviate some of these 'experience obstacles'.

Sometimes we take things for granted because we have been doing what we do for such a long time. Every interaction with our internal and external customers cannot NOT be an experience. The question becomes, "How

random or how managed is the experience that you offer?"
Incredible customer service will lead to a satisfied customer.
An incredible customer EXPERIENCE leads to satisfied,
LOYAL customers. Consider the experience!

"Growing Means *Learning to Work On Your Business
Not* In It" from an article in Forbes Magazine June of
2012 issue.

In this chapter, Jeff is describing the outcomes
of process improvement developed by observation
and feedback. This of course can be applied in any
project management environment. When was the last
time you took time to step back to took a look at the
customer experience of the interactions with your
project management and reporting style? This activity
is actually how exceptional service organizations get
to the point of 'rock star' delivery of experience. They
work 'on their business' and not just 'in their business'.
Why is project management any different? It's not.
But getting to 'rock star' status does not happen by
accident. It requires intentional focus on what will cause
people to snap their heads around and exclaim, "That
was awesome!"

Grow your PM business the same way. Make a list of
some things to try to increase your feedback loops from
stakeholders and customers. It will pay huge dividends,
so get started.

What Comes After the 'But'?

Becoming More Customer-Centric

Why is Starbucks so successful in selling you a $4.00 cup of coffee when MacDonald's charges $2.00?

Why does a stay at a Ritz Carlton hotel seem much different than at a stay at the Holiday Inn?

Most people today would answer that it's all about 'customer service' when, in fact, they would be wrong! Both MacDonald's and Holiday Inn offer incredible customer service. What Starbuck's and Ritz Carlton understand is that it is about the customer EXPERIENCE!

Throughout this book, we use the word 'customer' to make sure that, no matter what you do for a living, you understand that we all have internal and external customers. I would hope that everyone in your organization can define external customer. An Internal customer, however, is anybody without whom we can't do what we do every single day. This may be a paradigm shift for many of you. For example, my FedEx driver is an internal customer. If he doesn't show up on the days that I need him to pick up my parcels, I am out of business. So, he is a vital part of what I do every day.

So here is the problem on which this chapter is focused. Customer "*experience*" has become the new buzz word in the corporate world and I am not sure that most project management professionals really understand it. '*Service*' is what you offer your customers—internal and external—everyday as a trained professional; it is personal and it comes from the heart. It is the Project Manager who sees a team member struggling as a single Mom and finds a better day-care option for her. It is The Scrum Master who makes the coffee and cleans the team area before and after the daily stand-ups without recognition.

I am often asked if customer service is dead. It's not dead, but it is just not the differentiator it used to be. While your competitors are competing on service, why wouldn't you look to the next plateau—EXPERIENCE. Customer '*experience*' is about considering our customers' experiences from the minute they make contact with our organization until the minute they are done. This involves so many more people than just you.

Organizations or project teams that purposefully examine every customer *touch point*—those opportunities we have to touch the customer from the lobby security guard, to our on-hold message, to accounting, to our website to even how we report project status and results and many more—are those who will excel at the customer experience. By driving the message of the experience through every department, project phase or Sprint iteration, people realize that, no matter their title or contribution—part time or full time—they are part of the customer experience, they start to become more engaged. A 2013 study conducted by the Gallop organization, found that only 50% of Americans were engaged at what they do every day. That means that 50% of Americans come to work for a pay check or for the security. By having everyone consider their specific customer touch point and how they can better that one experience, they automatically become more engaged at what they do and ultimately, the customer is the one who benefits. Imagine a CPA meeting with a client (touch point) and hearing about a problem that's outside of their realm of expertise. They don't hesitate to suggest that someone else in the firm could help with that challenge. That CPA has just engaged that client at a whole different level because of taking advantage of one simple touch point.

The experience has to start with you! Because of your influence and because you touch so many different people at so many levels of the organization, you have to step up to the plate as the leader you are. It starts with you getting as many people as you can, walking around asking, *"What is the (fill in the name of your organization here) experience?"* Then, figure out how to shatter the stereotype of the experience customers EXPECT to have with you, your department or your organization. Ask yourself, *"What small touch point could I focus on*

this week that will ultimately shatter that stereotype?"
In an Agile environment this can be a focus of team
retrospectives. A retrospective is a time set aside at the
end of each Sprint to reflect on how the team can get
better or continuously improve its performance. How the
team delivers on its customer touch points can profoundly
impact the influence and success of the team. If time is not
set aside to consider these issues and opportunities they
will be lost in the furious delivery of project details and
never be addressed.

Imagine going to a new restaurant that has been
touted as the best in town. You arrive at 7:50 for an 8pm
reservation and are seated right on time. You go on to
have the best service and possibly the best food you have
ever eaten. At one point, the chef comes out to your table
and explains how each of your dishes was prepared. The
manager checks on you a few times. It is perfect. After
dinner, you proceed to go outside, you proffer your parking
ticket to the car valet and FIFTY FIVE MINUTES later
your car arrives! Isn't that part of the overall experience?
Of course it is. But, let's take this to the next step. It is now
3 months later and you have told hundreds of people to
go to that new restaurant because the food is amazing and
the service is outstanding. Then, you finish with one word.
BUT! *"...BUT your car will take forever to get to you
after dinner."*

What's this got to do with YOUR profession?
Everything! The minute we get our people asking *"What
comes after the but?"* is the minute we start to become

100% customer-centric. *"They are the nicest people to work with BUT they always are late on delivery".* *"You should call my lawyer because she is great BUT she charges too much.".* They are amazing care givers to my Mom *BUT* the place smells terrible. We need to examine every touch point and imagine what the customer might say. To start to make a shift from service to experience, begin by examining those touch points and see the world through THEIR eyes, not yours.

Bye! Bye! So Long! Farewell!

Who are your BEST customers?

So, who are your best customers? I'll argue they're your *lost customers.* No, the winter cold hasn't frozen my brain; I left out a key phrase. Who are your best customers - *to help you with business process and product improvement?*

Every business loses customers. It's a fact of business life. And the tendency may be, especially for the small businessperson, to shy away from communicating with customers who have walked away. Yet, consider what a treasure chest of information those lost customers hold. There's a reason those customers aren't buying from you. The reason may be benign. For example, they've moved or their needs have changed. But the reasons may be due to shortcomings in the way you do business or in the product or service they were buying from you. Wouldn't you like to know? Perhaps a minor correction would regain the customer.

Surprisingly, a lot of companies act as if they couldn't care less why customers are defecting. From a project management perspective these are the "Lessons Learned" that are talked about but rarely applied in the actual day-to-day delivery of the profession. How often are previous failed projects deconstructed to find the improvement nuggets that only show up in a failed project?

Let me give you a personal example. Almost two years ago I purchased an espresso maker for my wife for Christmas. Being tight with a buck, I bought a refurbished unit from Overstock.com. That winter, we did a kitchen renovation so certain less critical items got boxed away, including the espresso maker. After resurfacing, we used it for another month, until the pump failed. Technically, it was out of warranty, but I felt it was reasonable to at least ask for special consideration. I wrote to the customer service manager. No response. I wrote to the Director of Customer Satisfaction directly and through the web site "contact us" feature - they would not give me the name of any senior officer. No response. I tried to fax the German headquarters' customer service operation. The fax number on the web site didn't work. I posted the letter. No response. (I should add that Overstock.com did respond with a $20 credit although they had no compunction to do so.)

When my wife asked me last month why I hadn't just thrown out the now dust-covered espresso maker, I opted for one last shot. I went on line and found the name and address of the company president. I created a succinct

"Customer Centric Audit" pretending my experiences were part of an audit to measure how responsive Krups was to customers. (I explained the real situation in the Epilogue.) I printed it as a professional consultant's report and sent it Priority Mail.

About two weeks later, I received a call from the customer service manager I first tried to contact. She has offered to fix or replace the machine. More interestingly, *she thanked me for the feedback.* She could not find my original letter and was surprised at the trouble I had just getting some type of response. I intend to pursue those conversations later. Last week we received the repaired machine.

How many of your customers would go this far to voice a complaint? Not many! (I justify this tenacity in the name of research, which has a germ of truth due to my business practice and academic research.) Research has shown that customers are twice as likely to voice a complaint when provided a toll free number, and, of course, customer are most likely to complain if asked if there's a problem. Most important, customers who have had a complaint resolved effectively are more loyal than customers who have never had a complaint. That's the reason for creating service recovery programs.

Look at your own business or project and ask how easy you make it for customers to complain and what you do with complaint data. In other words, pretend you are a customer and do your own "customer-centric audit." Your company will fall into one of five distinct levels in complaint handling progression.

1. No response to complaints
2. Reactive response to complaints
3. Systematic response to complaints
4. Proactive complaint solicitation
5. Feedback to process or product owners for root cause correction

Note that these are cumulative. As you move through the successive stages, the customer receives some attempt at recovery, at first reactively and proactively, the company makes it easier to hear about complaints, and finally the full value of the complaint is leveraged through operational improvement.

Why is this important in project management? Because stakeholder management is increasingly important to the successful delivery of projects. As projects and project management offices become more and more strategic in their focus and purpose, this will be the leading edge of improvement for the project manager of tomorrow.

It's seems counter intuitive to *want* to hear more complaints, but we should! We can get more complaints by letting the customer know how to voice them. Toll free numbers and point-of-contact comment cards can work, but they're passive. Active solicitation of comments can best be done by contacting customers or stakeholders directly. Surveys after a completed transaction or scheduled meetings work best, depending upon the nature of your business. Today, it is important to have people who are dedicated to auditing comments about your company on social media. Responsiveness is a key to service recovery. If we wait too long, it becomes harder to resolve an issue.

The key is to let the customer know that you want their feedback –*and that you will act upon it.* That last point is key. If you don't provide service recovery and fix the underlying problem, the customer will be less likely to voice issues in the future. Also, remember to fix the problem *and* fix the customer. Included with our fixed espresso maker was a packing slip - no card or note. A small gesture could have remedied an upset customer's attitude.

A business of any size can do this. While there are technology tools, for example, CustomerExpressions.com or SpartaSystems.com, that can assist moving to stage 5, the heart of this program is simply executing a well-defined and well-conceived process. Get those complaints rolling in! You may be amazed at what you learn.

What the Group, "One Direction" Can Teach Us About Customer Experience

How EXPERIENCE Shapes Our Strategy

On a sticky July evening, the multimillion-selling vocal group One Direction ("1D") made a stop at the Izod Center in East Rutherford, NJ, on its international "Take Me Home" tour. The capacity crowd of 19,000+ fans, composed primarily of frenzied nine to sixteen year-old Jersey girls, welcomed the young UK stars with screams and open arms.

For those unfamiliar with the worldwide pop cultural impact of 1D, here's a quick summary:

The group's five members were originally contestants on the British version of "*The X Factor*" in 2010. They were signed to Simon Cowell's Syco Records (marketed and distributed worldwide by Columbia Records). Their first album, "Up All Night," was released in 2012, and their second album, "Take Me Home," came out in 2013. The group has sold 19 million singles and 10 million albums around the world.

Tickets for their tours sell out within minutes.

The passionate, emotional enthusiasm (and sizable financial expenditures) that 1D inspires among its massive global fan base is not a fluke: It's the result of a meticulously nurtured loyalty-building strategy that was on full display at the Izod Center on that July evening.

Companies that wish to develop positive connections with their own customers would be wise to learn from 1D's examples, which were carefully planned by their managers and flawlessly choreographed by the producers of their "Take Me Home" tour.

1. Deliver outstanding quality

One would expect 1D to put on an adequate show that pleased its young fans. But what happened at the Izod Center was a powerful spectacle that truly wowed the "Directioners".

Laser light effects. Explosions. Smoke. Confetti and streamers. Dazzling graphics and colorful, fast-paced videos on a wide, two-story screen behind 1D and the band. All were coordinated and displayed tastefully and impressively.

The Takeaway:

Every element of 1D's concert was calculated to dazzle its young fans/customers, and they all worked. Companies should aim to achieve such excellence in every aspect of their customer interactions by:

- Creating and delivering a first-rate product or service
- Providing courteous customer care
- Nurturing valuable dialogues and helpful social media interactions
- Crafting user-friendly multimedia sales and marketing collateral

2. Understand your customers' NGDs

The overriding NGD (need/goal/desire) for the majority of the Izod Center audience was to get closer than they had ever been before to their favorite 1D member (or, in the words of some of the young Directioners, to "breathe the same air as 1D").

1D served up the goods. Each member was featured, spotlighted, and called out throughout the show, giving their respective admirers plenty to shriek about.

And, in what was a brilliant move, the guys were attired in hip yet informal outfits: They didn't wear the glittery suits or elaborate costumes that boy bands of yore (e.g., Backstreet Boys, N' Sync, New Kids on The Block) sported when performing. This choice made the group's members more accessible (and attainable) to the shrieking tweens/teens.

The Takeaway:

One Direction's management and concert producers didn't create a concert experience that they thought would reflect their target consumers' NGDs; they created a concert experience that they *knew* would reflect their target consumers' NGDs.

Whether it was by research, observation, experience, or a combination of the three, the teams behind 1D's show succeeded because they had an accurate appreciation of what Directioners wished to derive from the group's live presentation.

Project managers should take this same approach when researching their own customers' specific NGDs. Rather than assuming or guessing, you should instead aim to learn exactly what the NGDs are and then reflect those in your opportunity, your product or your services.

3. Create real connections with your customers/members

One Direction bonded with Izod Center fans in three noteworthy ways. First, midway through the concert, the guys took a break from the music and invited the audience to send them tweets with questions about their tour. The fans' queries ("What's your favorite American food/TV show/etc.?") were posted on two massive video screens on either side of the main stage at the front of the arena.

After answering each tweeted question, the group then gave a shout-out to—and had a spotlight shined on—the section of the arena from which the question originated, sending the fans who were seated in that section into joyous hysterics.

Second, in sing-alongs and the call/response parts of songs that it performed throughout the night, 1D let the Jersey crowd know that they were the loudest and most enthusiastic audience on the tour. That incredible news made the arena's decibel level explode into the ear-bleed zone.

(One father told his daughter that 1D probably says the same thing to the audiences at each of its concerts, but she firmly insisted that 1D would never do that.)

Third, at numerous times throughout the evening, 1D members thanked the Directioners for coming to the show and let them know that the group would never have attained its current level of success—or had a chance to perform in New Jersey—if the fans hadn't been so supportive of their music and careers.

The Takeaway:

In each of the above examples, One Direction used the concert to establish powerful, memorable, and direct relationships with fans/customers. 1D also expressed tremendous gratitude to fans for the group's achievements.

Using social media channels, customer service channels (phone, chat, email), and email marketing efforts, you should seek to creatively connect and interact with your customers/prospects, as well as devise sincere ways to express their thanks for their support (e.g., purchases, referrals). Implemented correctly and genuinely, your multi-dimensional relationship-building efforts can yield significant customer loyalty, improved marketplace image, and future referrals.

4. Exceed your customers' expectations, then exceed them again

If One Direction had put on an energetic performance of fans' favorite songs, interacted with the audience, and enhanced the show with dynamic videos and explosive effects, the Directioners would have gone home very satisfied.

1D did that—and did so one better.

Just before the show's halfway mark, the group ascended stairs that led to a high platform above the floor of their stage. Each member attached a waist cable to his microphone stand. The elevated platform, which was tethered to an elaborate track apparatus that was bolted into the ceiling, began to slowly move from the front of the arena to the back—where it lowered the guys onto a second stage.

As the platform journeyed across the length of the Izod Center, the screams from the rear of the arena increased in volume. Fans in the faraway sections who previously had only been able to make out their favorite 1D members only via binoculars or on the giant video screens, were now closer to them than they could ever have imagined—or their seat locations suggested—they'd be.

Without doubt, that significant phone memory within the Izod Center was filled to capacity with photos and videos of this unexpected crowd-thrilling surprise.

The Takeaway:

To survive in the marketplace and keep up with your competitors, deliver what your customers expect. But to thrive in the marketplace and dominate your competitors, deliver more than what your customers expect. I have been saying it for years "Shatter the stereotype of the experience your customers EXPECT to have with you."

5. Surprise and innovate

A mom I spoke to said that she had heard 1D's albums played in their entirety by her daughter hundreds of times over the past year and that she knew all of the songs that the group sang at the show. One song, however, was unfamiliar.

Toward the end of the concert, One Direction performed a guitar-heavy, alternative rock-sounding song called "Teenage Dirtbag." The mom figured that she might have missed it when her daughter was listening to her albums, or maybe it had been released as a overseas single and hadn't been included on 1D's American releases. She asked her daughter when 1D had put the song out, and she didn't know. In fact, she had never heard 1D sing it before.

That "Teenage Dirtbag" was new to the young girl—and all of the Directioners at the Izod Center—didn't seem to matter: By the end of the second chorus, everyone was singing along. Elaborate graphics on the Izod Center video screens featuring the song's lyrics and 1D as comic book action heroes pretty much made the song theirs.

It turns out that "Teenage Dirtbag" was an alt-rock hit in 2000 by the band Wheatus. According to Billboard magazine, "Teenage Dirtbag" offered "keen melody, inventive production, and cool lyric about those who have felt like underlings during high school." Billboard went on to say that it "stands strongly on its own as an emphatic anthem and a song many teens will be proud to push hard from their car speakers."

The Takeaway:

1D's decision to create a version of "Teenage Dirtbag" was risky, unexpected, and absolutely brilliant. Whether it was a tease of its new album's sound, or a messaging tie-in with its anti-bullying partnership with Office Depot, or just something cool to perform live, "Teenage Dirtbag" was executed flawlessly—and the group's fans/customers loved it.

You should strategically embrace similar boldness and innovation to surprise your customers and the marketplace. It's easy to coast when a successful formula is discovered. It takes guts and a long-term perspective to intelligently expand on that formula in a way that will please current clients and attract prospects.

1D's success is no accident. It's the well-planned result of the band's charisma and talent combined with excellent songwriting/production, spectacular marketing, and—perhaps most important—impeccable customer experience.

> Every 1D concert is a project as is the construction of the tour itself.
> Whenever we take on a new project, the first thing we do is work on the definitions; Why is this project being proposed? What is the vision it is trying to fulfill? What is the expected business value that will be derived from the successful delivery of this project? Who cares and why? There is a string of pertinent questions that should be considered every time a project is initiated that, once considered and answered,

will make the project stronger and easier to manage and deliver. We do it with a simple framework we call the Unified Vision Framework. This framework has a number of models and methods (which can be seen in depth in Ted's book co-written with his brother Andrew "The Nehemiah Effect: Ancient Wisdom from the World's First Agile Projects") but the core revolves around the Four Ds and VSPT. The Four Ds are; Define, Distill Agreement, Deliver, and Drive Success. VSPT is Vision, Strategy, People and Tasks. You can deconstruct the above example and the 5 areas Jeff outlined by asking questions using this framework. You will quickly see the important project milestones and touch-points and also see how customer feedback from past projects informed changes to current project delivery.

For example, where do you think the moving set idea came from? Either some other entertainer did it with huge success or someone on the project team for 1D came up with the concept, tried it and tweaked it to the point it is now a crowd pleasing part of the show today. In other words, someone somewhere on a project team got creative in the delivery of the project result and the project Sponsor or Product Owner said yes to the change, to the delight of current and future concert attendees.

If you are leading a project there are things that can be done to improve the customer experience or the team experience, but it will take someone (that would be you) initiating the space and time for creativity and innovation to surface.

You may have had an idea pop into your head even as you read this section. Write it down and think through what steps you could take tomorrow to make it happen. Let your team beat it up and improve it. Start making space for creativity and watch your team and your project results improve. It will happen.

My Pizza Joint is YOUR competition!

Knowing Your Market
Better than Anyone Else

I am not a pizza-eater! I think I got *pizza'd* out in college. Typically, my family will save their pizza cravings for when I am out on the road and not able to complain that I have nothing to eat.

One evening, my wife called me in a frenzy—late from work. She is a mediator by profession and is one of the best 'closers' I know. She reasoned, "If you don't want to order a pizza and find something else for you to eat, then you can make dinner for everyone." I asked the only logical question, "Who do I call to order pizza?"

I found the number to Mama Leone's Pizza—apparently my family's favorite—on a magnet on our refrigerator. After two rings, the phone was answered. "Mama Rocks Pizza. Welcome to the Tobe household!" Now, I am very familiar with caller ID, so I wasn't shocked that the young man knew who was calling. What did surprise me was the fact that he pronounced my name correctly. Most people say 'Tobey' on their first attempt, not the correct pronunciation. Good guess? I wasn't sure.

The voice on the other end continued, "Who am I speaking to this evening?" I replied, "This is Jeff Tobe…" He interrupted, "Oh, Mr. Tobe. You've never called before!"

Ok. I am also familiar with databases, but I must admit that I was intrigued. The voice continued, "Will it be the regular tonight?".

To prove how bizarre a thinker I am, I must admit that it immediately dawned on me that I didn't want to give this guy the information. Remember, my family orders pizza while I am away. I want HIM to tell ME what the 'regular' is. If it isn't what my family should be ordering, then I want to know who is ordering pizza from my house when I am not there!!

"You tell me what you think the *regular* is," I challenged. He didn't hesitate in replying, "1/2 pepperoni…1/2 plain cheese!" He was right.

It was his next question that sent me reeling. "Mr. Tobe, have you fixed the light on your front porch?"

Understand that my wife had been pestering me for over 2 months to change the light bulb in that fixture, but it is up high and I have to get the ladder… You get the picture! More interesting, however, was that this guy asked the question. I could only ask him why. He continued, "The last time we delivered a pizza, your light was burned out and my driver had trouble reading your house number. I don't want your pizza to arrive to you cold."

"It will be fixed by the time you get here," was all that I could blurt out!

The point of this insight into the Tobe pizza-ordering-realm? This pizza—according to my family—is not the best tasting pizza in town. But, would we order from anyone else? I doubt it. You see, it has nothing to do with the product, but everything to do with the buying experience.

I have considered this the essence of a successful organization for a long while. It is no longer 'customer service' that sets us apart from our competition. It is the 'customer experience' that will give us the competitive edge. Think about paradigm-shifting organizations like

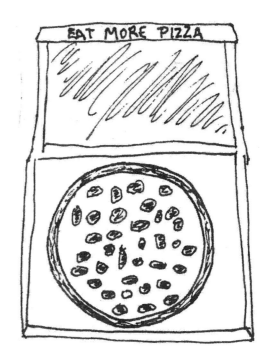

Saturn, Nordstrom, Cheesecake Factory, and, yes, Mama Leone's Pizza. They do not offer the best product or service. Nor are they just customer service-oriented. They offer a unique customer experience.

Consider the experience your customer has with you. It is the overall impression they have AFTER the transaction is complete. Would they recommend you to others? Do they become what Ken Blanchard calls, "Raving fans", or are they simply satisfied with your customer service? Service, by the way, is simply <u>expected</u> in today's environment. No, things have to go deeper. Beyond service is the emotions I experience during and after our interaction.

My friend at Mama Leone's knew us better than any other pizza joint I could call. He asked the right kinds of questions to ensure that we would call only them the next time we wanted to order pizza. By the way, it turns out that the light fixture on our front porch did not simply need a light bulb, but needed a more complicated 'fix' that I could not provide. So, what did I do? I stood outside with a flashlight and waited for the driver to arrive! Now that's what I call an 'experience'.

"There are three Business Personalities: Entrepreneur, Manager, Technician"

Michael Gerber in "The E Myth

Last year as the closing Keynote for THE Project 2014 (an intercollegiate project management competition hosted and run by the Western Michigan Chapter of PMI) Dr.

James Brown made the following suggestion, "If you want to get better as a project manager read books on sales." There were a lot of confused PMs after that comment. The thought was 'we manage projects, we do not sell things'. But Dr. Brown's point is spot on. PMs do indeed sell. Every time they interact with a team member or stakeholder or customer they are (or should be) in a sales mode. Selling what? The vision and ultimate value of the project deliverables. Sound advice, Dr. Brown!

So, why the quote from Michael Gerber above? The E Myth is a book about what it takes to make it as an entrepreneur and why so many good technicians or managers fail at running a business. They know the technical details, or have managed aspects of a project or business, but never made the transition to the mindset needed to succeed in business. Many PMs suffer from this same malady. They are good at the technical delivery or management aspects of project management but never linked their activity to the higher purpose of the organization and how their project fulfills that purpose. They never fully investigate or own the "why".

Jeff's pizza company owned the "why" and delivered an experience that exceeded his expectations, thus making him a fan. It was still just pizza but the experience was handled in such a way that he knew they knew him and their business. It increased confidence and thus repeat sales.

We need the same intense focus on the "why" of a project so we can deliver in ways that cause confidence to rise within the team and the people and organizations we serve.

Know the "why" driving your team, stakeholders and customers. Find ways to translate that knowledge into an exceptional experience, and you will experience the same result Jeff's pizza company did ... repeat business.

How Well Do You Know Your Customer?

Do You Know Your Customers' Buying Styles?

On a recent cross-country trip, a flight attendant was very attentive to my needs. At one point, she flippantly remarked that I was a "high maintenance" passenger. After I got past my hurt feelings, it occurred to me that maybe she had more insight into her passengers than I had given her credit. When I pressed her for more information, I was surprised to find just how much she could teach me.

She explained that she and her colleagues actually could identify passenger "types" by the way they

161

handed in their cups and other trash, by the demands they made on them and generally by their willingness to chat, sleep or work. She went on to tell me that this was not in their official handbook, but that it came in very handy every single day. Before she left me pondering this unique approach to customer service, she added one more little ditty. She said, "If we get to know them, we can give them what they need before they even ask." What a simple but phenomenally insightful revelation. Do you know your clients' needs before they even ask?

If we are to be in complete control of the sales process, we need to first understand our own 'selling behavioral style' and second, find a way to quickly identify—and adapt to–any client's "buying behavioral style" as did the flight attendant. Psychologists have agreed for years that there are basically four different 'behavior styles' in western society. These styles have been called so many different things by so many studies, tests and instruments, but the fact remains that they all agree on the number four. The one study that I use in all of my sales training, was promoted by then Carlson Learning Company (now, Wiley/Inscape Publishing) out of Minneapolis and is referred to as DiSC©. From the matrix below, try to identify your dominant style and keep in mind the following principles:

- We all have each of the 4 tendencies, but we are dominant in one
- No one style is better than the others

- We are examining only your "work behavioral style". You have other 'styles' at home, at play, as a parent etc.

Let's take a look at how to handle each behavioral style in a sales situation.

Dominant

Clients with a high Dominant style–or a High D—are probably the easiest to recognize in a group situation. They thrive on being in control and will usually ask you to "get to the bottom line". They are seldom concerned with details as long as you can provide what you promise. Because the High D is so task-oriented, you should always talk about the results they will achieve by using your product or service. Always be prepared and look professional with this style. As a matter of fact, I suggest that when working with someone you don't know, always treat them like a High D. This way you can't go wrong. I have never encountered a person who complained that a project manager got down to business too quickly, but I have met many who rued the days they encountered professionals who insist on chatting.

By the way, I especially enjoy doing business with a High D. They are less likely to be concerned with price and, of the four styles, are quickest to make a decision. They tend to be very loyal clients, until you make one mistake; then they will hunt you down and kill you! Remember, this person needs to be in control, but are concerned with time restraints, so only give them two or three choices. Finally, do not try to use incentives or "specials" or gimmicks with a High D. They just don't get excited about them and, even worse, it makes you less professional in their eyes.

Influence

From my sales training experience, I would venture to guess that the majority of salespeople in the western hemisphere fall under this category. High I's are also very easy to recognize because of their ability to be excellent communicators, friendly and highly social. You will know you are working with a High I because they will generally want to get to know you a little better. They may suggest meeting over lunch or on the links. Influencers love to generate enthusiasm and, unlike High D's, are very people-oriented rather than task-oriented. If you ask them why they enjoy their work, they will tell you that it has something to do with the people they get to meet and the fun that they have. When you are working with this style, make sure you emphasize how your solution will make them look great to the people with whom they work. Emphasize the fun they will have or the enjoyment they will get. High I's love "specials" or incentives; especially if it means some type of personal recognition or gain.

The challenge you have in dealing with a High I is that you may have trouble keeping their interest when it comes to details. My suggestion is to put all the details in writing after your meeting. High I's are often so disorganized that you can't count on them to remember the facts. When approaching the Influencer, remember to show them testimonials of other recognizable clients who have benefited from your solutions; they love to be in good company. Do not give Influencers a lot of choices as it will just confuse them. Present your <u>one</u> best solution with lots of enthusiasm and remember to allow enough time for socializing.

Steady

Another very people-oriented style is our Steady buyer or our High S. Unlike our Influencer style, the High S professional does not like to change too quickly and will take a little more convincing to do so. The High S has traditional values and is motivated by personal stability, so we must approach them with a "soft sell". If you are a High D or a High I, you need to calm down and take it slow and easy with your High S client. Your enthusiasm or penchant for wanting to quickly get to the bottom line will simply turn off this person. The High S style has a knack of taking ideas and putting them into motion, so they are a great person to have on your side. You must provide this person with guarantees of minimum risk. Your solution, including incentives, must be oriented to how it will make the whole department or company look good; remember they are concerned with the "team" effort. Although they may seem slow to change, simply provide them with proof on why a change will be advantageous and, most importantly, show them how your solution will make things run "smoothly". The High S buyer is concerned with how your solution will be implemented, so provide details in this area along with a plan on how problems will be corrected. If you want to begin to get on the good side of a High S, simply compliment them on their family; you will find photos all over their office!

Conscientious

The fourth style is motivated by accuracy in achieving their goals. Recognizing this, successful project managers orient their solutions to providing details as to why theirs is the "correct" answer to the challenge. You must expect a slower decision cycle with our High C professionals because they need "just one more study" or "one more opinion" before they sign on the dotted line. Like our Dominant style, High C's are very task-oriented and are not interested in socializing. Show them that you have analyzed and prepared your solution. High C's will want to spend time with you going over the details and checking for accuracy. (I recently had a prospect return a proposal so that I could correct the 'typos' in the copy!) When presenting ideas to a High C, slow down, put all details in writing and don't exaggerate. They are not so concerned with quantity of solutions as with quality. You must be patient and persistent. You will recognize your High C person when you receive a phone call from them, eight months after your initial presentation, and they inform you that they are ready to move forward. The problem is that if you are a High D or a High I, you have already erased them from your data bank and written them off as hopeless! Finally, when working with a High C, establish your credibility by offering both the pros and cons of your solution. If you don't, they will!

> *"If you have anything valuable to contribute to the world, it will come through the expression of your own behavior—that single spark of divinity that sets you off and makes you different from every other living creature."*
>
> Bruce Barton

It is only natural that our main interest is what we learn about OUR style. Still, we need to remember that understanding our client's style and being able to adapt to their preferences, will not only simplify the process, but set us apart as a true project management professional. We can see that each behavioral style has definite strengths and admirable qualities. Before you can collaborate effectively and productively with your clients—before you can establish any kind of relationship with them—they need to know that you recognize these qualities in them. By showing your client that, in spite of your differences, you understand, appreciate and even value their individual behavioral strengths, you build a ground work of mutual trust and respect. Then, and only then, may you anticipate their needs before they express them.

"Whether you are a top executive, a middle manager, a first-line supervisor, an accountant, or a secretary, your success depends largely on your ability to deal with other human beings."

From *Social Style / Management Style: Developing Productive Work Relationships* by Doctors Robert and Dorothy Bolton.

The above quote could obviously be crafted for project managers. A large part of dealing with people is observing and knowing where their comfort zones are. This is what Jeff is describing in this chapter.

The Social Style concept (which is laid out here by Jeff) was first formulated by David Merrill and his associates in the mid-nineteen hundreds. Wilson Learning adopted his material in training sessions that I participated in during the Fall of 1979. It has helped me greatly over the years.

There are many variations of this concept now from DiSC™ (Jeff's material in this chapter comes from the DiSC™ system) to Meyers Briggs among others. I would strongly suggest if you are involved in project management to get into one of these types of training sessions. It will help you expand as a leader and as a mentor of people. As Doctors Robert and Dorothy Bolton state on page 5 in the same book quoted above "Self-knowledge is the starting point of leadership effectiveness". As Machiavelli, the shrewd fifteenth-century author and statesman wrote, "To lead or attempt to lead without first having a knowledge of self is foolhardy and sure to bring disaster and defeat."

Bingo!

I will not repeat what Jeff has talked about here since you should be able to readily translate his thoughts into your PM situation. What I will say is your ability to flex, or enter into the comfort zone of the person you are dealing with, can make or break your interpersonal interactions. Here is a partial list of what is needed to flex into the various styles;

Dominant (High D or Driver)–
► Be on time
► Maintain strong eye contact
► Get to business
► Be short and specific
► Highlight results
► Be fast paced

Influence (High I or Expressive)–
► Be energetic
► Maintain strong eye contact
► Use stories
► Know the dream for the team and for the individual
► Emphasize the big picture first
► Be fast paced

Steady (High S or Amiable)–
► Listen!
► Affirm their ideas
► Be relaxed
► Invite their opinion
► Engage often and in person
► Use a slower pace

Conscientious (High C or Analytical) -
► Be on time
► Give facts
► Use fewer stories
► Be more formal in your approach and conduct
► Do not exaggerate
► Allow their speed

The Bolton's say this about flex, "Style flex is the employment of appropriate interpersonal processes to achieve desirable outcomes." In other words, you can increase your effectiveness by paying attention to how others would like to be approached.

In his longer workshops, Jeff likes to point out that we now have to "communicate with people in a way in which they need to be communicated to, NOT the way we have always communicated with them". This is so true and is at the heart of the Bolton's book and my own presentations including "Think Like a Duck". Basically, it is paying attention to how any stakeholder or team member or customer is hearing what you are trying to communicate. So, if it looks like a duck, walks like a duck and quacks like a duck you should probably communicate with it like a duck. It will increase your effectiveness … guaranteed.

(The following chapter was included in the original "Coloring Outside the Lines" book. Most project managers tell me they are NOT in sales! We disagree, but that is a topic for another day. We chose to leave this chapter in because of the moral of the story which, we think you will agree, is very applicable...)

Salesperson Appreciation Day

How Creativity and Sales Go Hand-in-Hand

I would like to suggest that we lobby whomever needs to be lobbied in Washington to establish an official Salesperson Appreciation Day! For one day each year, our clients would have to bow to <u>our</u> needs, jump when we say jump, and follow us around for one day telling us just how creative we really are. Only one piece of advice, "Don't hold your breath while we are trying to get this done"!

Short of a special day, I think it is important for all salespeople to stand back and give themselves a standing ovation once in awhile. In speaking to thousands of people every year in diverse professions, I have come to understand just how little innovate and creative salespeople are appreciated in our 'do-more-with-less' world.

Creativity in sales is the least appreciated, least understood of all our skills. And, in times of volatility and change, our most needed one.

Often, we fail to understand our own creativity because of the labels normally applied to the term. In one recent study, more than 130 buyers were asked to describe creative sales people.

They're "zany" or "artists," they said. They're "*off the wall.*" "*Creative sales people are hard to manage, difficult to nail down; they like to make their own rules.*"

Creativity, at least in terms of sales importance, can be much more clearly defined. I believe that creativity and resourcefulness are much the same thing. Resourcefulness is the trait we must develop in ourselves if we want control over the sales situation. If we examine the word resourcefulness, we see that it is little more than creativity: The ability to bring something into existence that does not yet exist, the skill of dealing with any kind of sales challenge.

Harry Pickens, a professor at University of Florida, put it best in a keynote address I once attended when he talked about seeing the 'invisible'. Our ability in any profession to see opportunities where others see limitations is what defines success. If we don't appreciate our creativity, our clients certainly can't be expected to.

While sitting in the lobby of a hotel in Orlando, I struck up a conversation with a woman who proudly told me that she was an event planner. She explained that she was new to the profession and new to sales. Her background was actually in accounting. She was middle-aged, lived in a small mid-western town with her husband and two kids. She was about as far from "zany" as you can get.

But, when she spoke about her new career, her creative resourcefulness came through loud and clear. Bobbi had lost her job several months before and soon after, decided to work closer to home. "I was tired of commuting," she explained. "It's worth a drop in salary not to have to go into the city every day."

With her husband, Bobbi spent a weekend driving around some of the new commercial areas within a certain radius of their home, noting the names of larger companies. She began applying to these firms. One, in particular, captured her fancy—a growing special events company.

At first, Bobbi approached the company in a traditional way. She sent a resume and followed up with a phone call. To the company's credit, they had decided that they were no longer going to hire 'anyone who breaths and can sell', and they politely explained that they had no need for a numbers person in the firm at that time.

Not to be discouraged, she took a different tack. Checking business directories, Bobbi found the name of the owner of the company. Rather than just make your traditional cold call, Bobbi started asking everybody she knew whether or not they had done business with this person. She found out that her baby-sitter's mother was a copier salesperson and had just sold the firm a new copier. Bobbi spoke to the woman, trying to gain some insight into the owner's mindset. She found out that the owner was very progressive and valued 'creativity.'

Bobbi called the owner directly and simply explained how 'creative' she had been in getting to him; resourcefulness at its best. The owner agreed to meet with her and hired her on the spot. I can only guess that he recognized the opportunity to hire someone, no matter their background, who had the drive and *resourcefulness* to get what they wanted.

I asked Bobbi, "Have you always been creative like this?"

"Creative?" Bobbi replied, puzzled. "I think of it more as determined." She chuckled. "I'm certainly not creative."

UGH! This is what tears at my very being. If we can't appreciate our own creativity, innovation and resourcefulness, how can we expect our clients to?

What you must realize is that dogged determination is necessary to overcome obstacles that normally stop other people. There is a true creative force in salespeople like Bobbi. Their willingness to see beyond the obstacles allows them to use their imagination to conjure up solutions that have never existed before.

Every day should be our own 'Salesperson Appreciation Day.' Why wait for our clients to declare it? It may never happen. It has to start with you.

"A 2013 report from the Oxford Martin School concludes that 45 percent of American jobs are at high risk of being taken by computers (AI and robots) within the next two decades."
    From page 62 of *Bold: How to Go Big, Create Wealth and Impact the World* by Peter Diamandis and Steven Kotler.

The salient point in this Chapter, is that, for Bobbi, determination was not seen as creativity. At times the tenacity of a project team to break through the impediments to find a solution and deliver the project deliverables is amazingly creative. Many times the team just sees it as 'we saw a problem and found a way around it to accomplish our objective'. Exactly! Innovative problem solving will always be needed and always be in demand, and good PMs excel at this.

The quote above from Bold is reflective of the disruption that has been happening in our economy over the past few years. Tectonic shifts have occurred and massive changes are hitting us on a weekly basis. This rapid pace of change is not likely to diminish any time soon and thus sustains the need for project managers who tenaciously focus on solutions with their team, breaking through barriers to deliver successful outcomes. Robots will never facilitate the internal unity needed to foster a high-performing team. Project managers will be holding those reins and it is imperative that project managers be aware of their impact and value. We should indeed hold that ability in high esteem and have a project manager appreciation day as well.

Who is bringing the cake?

Frequent Flier Pointers

Four Lessons We Need to Know About Our Clients

If, like myself, you are a 'road warrior' and you play the frequent flier game, you can appreciate how frustrating it is to have to travel on one of those _other_ airlines. You know! The one where you have no status. Where you are treated like a plebian and you look for horror stories to relate to your friends. Awhile back, I looked forward to the unpleasant duty of having to fly on one these inferior lines in order to make a connection to another city.

Now, I also must share with you that, if given the choice, I prefer to travel cross-country in very comfortable clothing. It is not unusual to find me in jeans, a golf shirt and sneakers. On the day of this 'flight into the unknown", I arrived at the airport dressed in this fashion.

I finally made it to a ticket agent, after having to wait in the 'commoner's line', and was greeted by an abnormally large smile on a woman in about her late 50's. The first words out of her mouth? *"Guess you're not used to having to wait in line?"* I was skeptical as to why she said that. I certainly didn't think I looked the part of a person not used to being kept waiting. She noticed my inquisitive look and she drew my attention to the luggage tag on my briefcase now sitting on the counter in front of her. It indicates that I am the top 'tier' of my preferred airline. "What can we do to make you change that tag to one of ours by the end of this year?"

Lesson number one—*Do any of us take the time to look for indications that our customers are already loyal to one of our competitors?* Do we then take this information and process it to our advantage? This woman had a choice. She could have dismissed me as one of 'their' customers or she could take this one opportunity— without having a second chance as far as she knew—to convert me to their product or service.

I found it difficult to answer her question concerning how they could win my loyalty. I was very fond of my airline. And I know the hassles and tribulations one must go through to begin a new frequent flier program anew. I looked at her and sheepishly shrugged my shoulders.

Lesson number two—Do you understand the huge discrepancy between what your prospective client perceives as the *cost* of doing business with you versus the *value* of doing business with you? Remember, this is not reality— this is *their* perception. We must see the world through our clients' eyes to see the way our client buys.

Almost as if she had read my mind, the woman allayed my fears. *"I can imagine how the thought of starting all over with a new airline must paralyze a lot of frequent travelers like you. I would like you to give us a fair try. Would it help if I offered you an upgrade to first class on this cross-country trip?"*

Now, as many of you professionals are aware, First Class is a self-indulgence afforded to us by our airline because of our status, but not one for which I would consider paying on any carrier. I turned to my new friend and graciously accepted her offer while biting my tongue in glee. She floored me with her next request. *"Unfortunately, we have a dress code in our First Class cabin,"* she explained. Seriously?

She proceeded to walk out from behind the counter and survey me from head to foot. With an unapologetic look she continued, *"If you would be willing to change into something a little more professional, I would be glad to upgrade you."*

What's one to do? Compromise one's very comfort? Acquiesce to such an obviously insane dress policy? *Absolutely!* I asked where the nearest men's room was located and told her to hang on to her upgrade. Within 3 minutes I was back, having fulfilled my part and waiting to consummate the deal. True to her word, she handed me a shiny new folder—the one that proudly displays the words FIRST CLASS on the outside—and I proudly proceeded to my gate.

Lesson number three—*ASK!* How many opportunities have we missed because we did not ask? If our clients want something from us that badly, we can basically ask them to do what it takes to get it. Once we understand who it is with whom we are dealing, it puts us in the proverbial driver's seat.

Last week I was flying on my original airline once again (it takes time for the 'weaning' process!). I struck up a conversation with my seatmate—in first class of course! With his baby finger extended as he sipped his tea, he explained to me that he too 'endured' that other airline just the week before and was abhorred by their lack of customer service. Before I could defend my new friends, he finished with, *"They do tell a good story however. The woman at the ticket counter told me that she once actually got some guy to change his clothes just to get*

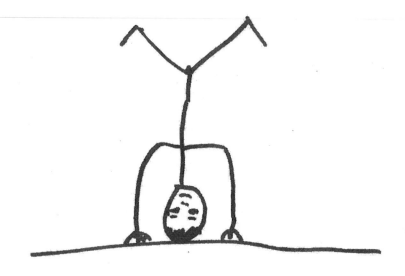

an upgrade. Can you imagine being that desperate to fly first class?"

Lesson number four—It's all in your perspective. I sat there thinking to myself that this guy didn't even know the half of it! Had the ticket agent asked me to be loyal to them for the next three months *and* stand on my head, I probably would have done that as well.

> "At the core, strategy is about focus, and most complex organizations don't focus their resources. Instead they pursue multiple goals at once, not concentrating enough resources to achieve breakthrough in any of them."
> *Good Strategy, Bad Strategy* by Richard Rumelt.
>
> I do not know if the airline gate agent in Jeff's story understood the overarching purpose, mission or vision of her organization. However, I do know that she exhibited an intense focus on a known value to her company—moving a business traveler from one airline to another. She observed the tag identifying Jeff as a top level member of a competing airline and offered a perk similar to what he would have obtained had he been on his preferred carrier as a way to demonstrate service and nudge him toward considering a change. Brilliant!
>
> She was asking questions in her mind as Jeff walked up to the counter. This resulted in her verbal inquiry. You can do the same. Ask questions.
>
> Dr. Rudolf Flesh in his book *"The Art of Clear Thinking"* gives us a list of questions as a starting point;
>
> - What am I trying to accomplish?
> - Have I done this sort of thing before? How? (sounds like lessons learned)

- Could I do it some other way?
- How did other people tackle this?
- What kind of person or persons am I dealing with?
- How can this situation be changed to fit me?
- How can I adapt myself to the situation?
- How about using more? Less? All of it? Only a portion? One only?
- Two? Several?
- How about using something else? Something older? Something newer? Something more expensive? Something cheaper?
- How near? How far? In what direction?
- How soon? How often? Since when? For how long?
- Could I do this in combination? With whom? With what?
- How about doing the opposite?
- What would happen if I did nothing?

This interesting list was compiled and published by this Harvard professor in 1951. In other words, asking questions is nothing new. It is still effective and maybe this list will inspire you to a develop better list of questions you can ask related to your project or your project deliverables, or a situation you may be facing right now that needs a creative kick to pull it out of the ditch.

Ask questions and act on the hunch.

Dr. Rumelt's quote above is more the norm. People do not ask enough questions and also do not have an understanding of the corporate vision and its strategic paths to success. They are focused on task level delivery of items they are given. The person in Jeff's story moved beyond the norm and caused a possible disruption and re-consideration by a potential future high value customer. It is known as disruptive thinking. Without the vision and the focus this will not happen.

Peter Drucker once stated, "Only three things happen naturally in organizations: friction, confusion, and underperformance. Everything else requires leadership." This Agent by acting showed leadership.

So how does this apply to project management? Know the purpose, mission and vision of your organization better than anyone else in the company. Memorize the published strategic initiatives that the executive team has decided are important in translating the vision into reality. Link your project and your project team to those known items and keep them visible constantly. Continuously ask questions. Your leadership in knowing and implementing these items will cause Mr. Drucker's identified friction, confusion and underperformance to cease and high performance to win the day.

Motivation Is Us!

Five Truths That Prevent You From Motivating Others

In these downsized times, the number one question I get asked by managers in any industry is, "How do we motivate our people or our clients and keep them motivated to stay on schedule or on budget or on task?" I have thought a lot about motivation because it is not uncommon for someone to introduce me as a *'motivational'* speaker. Something about that appellation has bothered me since I first got into professional speaking and something about being asked how to motivate people has also been a tough quandary. Then it struck me one day during a 3-day training session with a large promotional products distributor...

> *You can't motivate your people any more than you can motivate your clients to buy into your ideas!*

1. You cannot motivate other people!

> *Motivation is a fire from within. If someone else tries to light that fire under you, chances are it will burn very briefly.*
>
> Stephen Covey

What we have to realize is that we can give people incentives to perform better and encourage and support their efforts, but the basic motivation for their behavior must come from within. People motivate themselves. All we can do as a manager or as a client is to create an environment that aids in motivating someone to do something. For example, I recently spoke to one of the project managers at a large corporation in Cleveland Ohio. She explained to me that her boss was a wonderful man who kept her motivated at all times. Knowing what I have discovered, I probed deeper and found that, in fact, the boss just understood his people's individual likes and dislikes and structured an environment around those things that turned on his people. Posters around the office, an open door policy and a 'bi-annual customer focus group' added to creating that environment that is essential for people to motivate themselves. How can you create the environment to motivate yourself?

2. All people are motivated!

This is probably the most controversial thing I share with people around the world. Most of you probably know someone that you feel just isn't motivated at all. Maybe it's one of your clients with whom you just can't find the right 'button' to push. Maybe it's a co-worker with whom you have tried dangling the proverbial 'carrot' with no response.

Actually, research indicates that *all people are motivated*, no matter how they're behaving! Say, for example, Joan is working at a slow pace. Her manager may assume Joan is lazy or 'unmotivated'. But she actually may be motivated by a desire to achieve perfection. If the task requires speed instead of perfection, Joan's manager needs to coach her to help her adapt her behaviors, but there is no need to motivate her. Even when someone is inactive, they are still motivated. In this case, they are motivated to do nothing!

3. People do things for their reasons, not yours!

Getting down to the nitty-gritty, most people are motivated by unconscious motives most of the time.

                                                        Richard J. Mayer

Although this may seem selfish, we have to realize that self-interest is simply a question of survival for many colleagues and clients. Even if we can't directly motivate others, we can better relate with people if we approach them with the desire to find out their reasons for doing what they do—or not doing what you would like them to do. In this new 'relationship' world in which we operate, putting yourself in the client's shoes will better help you understand their reasons for behaving the way they do. There is a saying that I share in all of my training; *"See the world through your client's eyes and you'll see the way your client buys!"*

4. A person's attributes—when overused—can become a detriment!

Tom, a computer programmer who attended one of my creativity workshops, related to me that he had recently received a promotion to division head. His analytical programming skills were highly touted throughout his international firm. In his new position, Tom applied the same painstaking care and deliberation to minor administrative issues as he did to his programming projects, and as a result, he was perceived as slow and often indecisive. Because of his tendency to research everything, some workers felt he didn't trust their judgment. His strength had definitely become a limitation. When dealing with certain clients, our strengths as sales people—ie. the gift of gab, the ability to chatter excessively—may just become our limitations even though that is what motivates us on a daily basis. Our role in this new relationship environment is to identify the *buying style* of our client and adapt to that. Fellow speaker and journalist, Jeffrey Gitomer says, *"People don't like to be sold but they love to buy!"* I tell salespeople all of the time to stop selling! Figure out how I buy and present your ideas, your service or your product to me in a way in which I will buy into it! Not in a way in which you are used to selling it.

5. If I know more about you than I have before, I can manage the sale

The business of expanding your consciousness is not an option. Either you are expandable or you are expendable.

Robert Schuller

This goes against the old credo, "Thou shalt not out-talk the project manager." As I share in my book, *The Sales Coach*, we need to ask more questions of those who work for us and of those who *buy* from us. We have to establish (and for many it's a case of re-establishing) our role as the seeker of information and the client's role as giver. Once we truly understand the power of controlling communication in creating a motivational environment, we can understand how we can also influence the entire process.

Many of us think we know ourselves pretty well, and yet we still are surprised by the way people react at times to the things we do or say. Our challenge is to recognize both our strengths and limitations so that we remain in control of our own motivation, particularly in those situations where we find ourselves typically uncomfortable or ineffective. We all know that we cannot change someone's behavior unless they are willing to change it themselves. When it comes to getting buy-in, we cannot change a client's motivation to agree or disagree, but we can simply provide them with an environment that makes it easier to do business with us over our competitors.

Is motivation permanent? I think Zig Ziglar, the guru of inspiration, answers that best:

"Of course motivation isn't permanent. But then, neither is bathing; but it is something you should do on a regular basis."

"The first responsibility of a leader is to define reality. The last is to say thank you. In between, the leader is a servant."

Max de Pree former CEO of Herman Miller.

"Lakhani and Wolf uncovered a range of motives, but they found that enjoyment–based intrinsic motivation, namely how creative a person feels when working on a project, is the strongest most pervasive driver" said Daniel Pink, referring to a study on why people contribute to open source projects without payment in his book "*Drive.*"

There are a number of elements needed to bring any team to a state of high performance and high creativity. The attitude and style of the project leader is one of the keys, if not the key element. Servant leadership has been discussed for many years and was highlighted by Jim Collins in his seminal book "Good To Great" as one of the key reasons companies moved from good status to great performers. The concept still holds true today.

Command and control attitudes kill motivation and creativity. Operating with high direction is an anti-pattern to high performance, and yet we see it over and over in organizations we are brought in to help. Typically, we see a strong desire to enact organizational change to improve performance but with little appetite for freeing people to decide freely on their own. You cannot have it both ways.

You may not be able to alter how your organization operates above you but you can change the atmosphere for your team. Here are some suggestions from Dan Rockwell's blog "Leadership Freak" on how to motivate people;

Pressure and coercion are like water to fire.

The need to pressure or coerce indicates *they're <your team> not interested*.

"Get past this notion that motivation is something that one person *does* to another...," Daniel Pink, author of, *Drive*, referring to a conversation with Edward Deci.

De-motivation and control:

Feeling controlled de-motivates. Pressure says you're in control and they aren't.

How do you feel when someone tries to control you? Do you calmly walk along or dig in your heels? It depends on how much power the controller has and how much you need the job. But, no one enjoys external pressure.

Make people feel powerless and they'll act like they're powerless.
The powerless always resist, eventually.

Five ways to motivate the unmotivated:

1. Reject the notion that motivation is something you do *to* others.
2. Give power, don't take it. Power enables control. Control engages. Feeling controlled disengages.
3. Put more in if you want more out. Train, develop, and release. Proficiency enables action; incompetence blocks it.

4. Tap their interests. You don't have to pressure people to do what interests them.
5. Connect don't disconnect. Build relationships. Connecting with others and organizations motivates the unmotivated.

Motivation is an observational art form. You need to observe the needs of your team and find ways to assist them in filling or fulfilling those needs as a servant leader.

Servant leadership is a powerfully effective method in motivating any team. People are motivated to help leaders who have served them in real ways. It is how the game is played by some of the most successful people in the world. And, as Albert Einstein once said, "You have to learn the rules of the game. And then you have to play better than anyone else."

Play well.

It's Kind of Hard to Explain

People Do Business With People Who Seem to Love What They Do for a Living

Do you find it difficult to explain just what it is you do for a living sometimes? This has been a perplexing dilemma for me over the past 20 years until I traveled with my wife to Dallas years ago. I THINK I HAVE THE ANSWER, but first, let me fill you in on the earth-shattering experience that revealed this answer to me.

A few years ago, my wife and I were joined by friends of ours for dinner at a new restaurant in Dallas. These friends simply explained that they had been told that this new establishment had received rave reviews from everyone who had eaten there; they knew nothing else about it. The name of the restaurant? "ENIGMA".

Now, I pride myself on having a fairly a fairly extensive vocabulary, but the meaning of this word escaped me. I decided to check out a dictionary. The best explanation

I could find? *"Something that is difficult or hard to explain."*

What an odd name for a restaurant!

Before we were even seated, I knew that Enigma was going to be an eating experience we weren't soon to forget. With only about 10 tables, I understood why our friends had had to make reservations over one month prior to our arrival. My first observation was the outrageous decorations, including 10 tables that were completely different in design with no chairs that matched each other.

Our table was set with completely different dishes and silverware. I don't mean that each setting was different but that even at one place-setting none of the plates, none of the silver patterns, nor none of the glasses matched each other.

We ordered some 'adult beverages' and when they were delivered to our table we were amused at the fact that, although two of us had asked for the same drink, one glass was a regular 8 ounce water glass and the next was no smaller than a birdbath! Our server explained that it was simply 'luck of the draw' as to which glass you received.

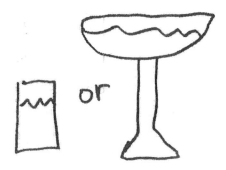

Next, our waitress handed each of us 3

different, very creative menus. Each of us had three different menus—12 menus total. We had to trade menus amongst the four of us to get an overall concept of the fare.

Besides the odd selections available on the menu, our waitress also explained that even if two of us ordered the same selection, she could not guarantee that they would come out prepared the same way. She could not even inform us of the side dishes that came with each selection. "This is why we are an enigma," she explained. "You have to give our chefs total creative freedom to prepare your meal."

She was absolutely correct. My wife's Mahi-Mahi came soaked in a wonderful green tamale sauce while our female friend's Mahi-Mahi arrived in a beautiful tureen blanketed with a white vegetable sauce. The rest of the meal was…it was…nothing short of an enigma!

Always in search of a great analogy to share with my audiences, by dessert I had had a mild epiphany! I knew the exact answer everyone is supposed to give when queried about what it is we do for a living. What I do is an *enigma*.

That's all you need to say to get someone's attention. When it comes to the creativity that you offer, the service or methodology you can customize and the challenges you can solve, it *should* be hard to explain. That's the lure!

The mystery surrounding this new explanation of your profession, may just be the thing that will attract customers, making <u>you</u> so popular that your calendar will be full. Every time they call you to ease a pain, they should have no idea what you are going to serve. They should however, sit back, enjoy the experience and trust that you will be creative each and every time they *experience* your expertise.

You see, it occurred to me that our job is not just to solve a business challenge but, like my dining adventure in Dallas, we must give our clients an <u>EXPERIENCE</u> every single time they require our expertise. Never give them the same menu when they ask you to wait on them. Never serve their solutions on the same plate or in the same glass.

Why fight it? What you do is probably an *enigma* and you should all be proud to demonstrate the mystery every time your client calls.

By the way, we paid more for our meal at Enigma than I have *ever* spent on dinner in my life! Do I care? Absolutely not. It was worth the experience. Is your client willing to pay for the 'experience' they have with you?

> "When all our enemies heard *of it*, and all the nations surrounding us saw *it*, they lost their confidence; for they recognized that this work had been accomplished with the help of our God."
>
> Nehemiah 6:16

The modern version of this ancient Hebrew text about the rebuilding of a 4.5 mile wall around the city of Jerusalem might read "Wow, how in the world did they do that?" This appears to be how Jeff and his wife reacted to their experience at the Enigma restaurant. While creating an experience might not be your idea of sound project management please do not dismiss the underlying truth here - different can be good.

"The Nehemiah Effect", co-written with my brother Andrew, is not a religious book. It is a deconstruction of how an amazing project, completed 2,500 years ago, utilized Agile practices to accomplish its goal. The result of this 'you should not have been able to do that' project outcome was recognized by the wider community as unusual and excellent. It set the stage for future success as well.

Nehemiah did not follow the known construction practices of his day. He approached the situation differently. He had to organize over 50,000 volunteers with a crew of 150 leaders he brought with him in a very short period of time due to the unrest in the region. His vision was clear. His authority and leadership were established. His priorities were narrowed. His cycles were short and visible. His communication system was simple and highly effective, and he fostered and nurtured the potential intrinsic motivation that the situation provided. All of these items worked together to create a very large yet high-performing team. The delivery was a project result that even today is recognized as awesome. He approached the project with a different mindset and led the team to deliver above and beyond any reasonable expectation of success. You can do the same.

Look at your project through a different lens. Approach it differently. Be a modern Nehemiah and deliver outstanding results.

There is a PM who decided to change his image, to make himself memorable in his huge organization in a positive way. He started wearing bow ties. Every day he showed up for work in a long sleeve shirt, dress slacks and a bow tie. The result? Even people who did not know his name knew who the "bowtie guy" was. It quickly set him apart from the crowd. He was recently promoted to a much better higher paying position. Yes, different can be good.

Listen to Your World...

Effective Listening Techniques to Make You a Better Management Professional

I want to share with you the number one, outside-the-lines, only-found-here, sure- to-make-you-a-million, management technique that until now has remained a mystery to most project managers. Those rare people who have discovered this one "tool" have gone on to change the world as we know it.

Now, it is going to require most of you to get outside of your comfort zone to be willing to try something that does not come naturally for most business professionals. When we concentrated on this in our business, it increased our sales, changed the way we worked with each other and just made us more appealing to our clients. What is it you ask? It's our ability to listen!

You may not have realized that listening is such an important, yet often overlooked, business skill. We spend 70 percent of our waking hours in verbal communication. Listening, as a method of taking in information, is used far more than reading and writing combined. Isn't your job—no matter the industry—to listen; to process what we hear and then to react?

An informal definition of listening is simply, *taking in information from our consumers while remaining non-judgmental and empathetic.* It involves acknowledging the consumer in a way that invites the communication to continue by providing limited, but encouraging input, carrying an idea one step forward.

The challenge we have is that when we think about listening, we tend to assume it is basically the same as hearing. This is a dangerous assumption because it leads us to believe effective listening is instinctive. As a result, we make little effort to learn or develop listening skills and unknowingly neglect a vital function of communication that results in miscommunication and ultimately loss of market share. To paraphrase Dr. Stephen Covey author of

7 Habits of Highly Effective People, *"One of the basic of all human needs is to understand and to be understood."* Our clients need to know that we understand their concerns and needs.

Let's look at seven techniques to becoming a better listener. Although these focus on the literal aspects of the personal listening process, I have prompted you to think about how they apply to your marketing and sales challenges as well.

1. Listen with your Eyes and your Ears

Many times someone's body is telling much more than their words. Many studies have been conducted in this area, and most concur that the words that we use in communicating with each other account for less than 10 percent of our total message. The tone of our voice accounts for somewhere around 30 percent, and our body language makes up about 60 percent of our message.

ARE YOU ACTUALLY WATCHING FOR YOUR CUSTOMER'S REACTIONS TO YOUR COMPANY'S 'BODY LANGUAGE' OR ARE YOU SIMPLY LISTENING TO THEIR WORDS?

2. Never Interrupt

Interrupting another person does not necessarily involve speaking up at an inappropriate time. We interrupt others when we argue mentally with something that is said, when we disagree with a point that is made or when we allow our minds to wander. Even if the purpose of your communication is to present information or describe your services, try to do less than 50% of the talking. Most of what you say should be in the form of questions to prompt the client to give you more information—not to be seen as an interruption. Once the other person perceives you to be competing with them to speak, they may become too uncomfortable to give you the real message. As a rule of thumb, before speaking, pause and count to five after the other person stops talking.

ARE YOU <u>ASKING</u> YOUR CUSTOMERS FOR THEIR FEEDBACK WITHOUT INTERRUPTING?

3. Ignore Distractions

We are perceived as being an empathetic listener when we learn to ignore distractions of any kind. We have to visually mentally and emotionally focus on the speaker. Listen with your eyes, ears and heart. Tell yourself, "I'll listen to this person only."

DO YOUR CLIENTS TRULY BELIEVE YOU ARE LISTENING TO JUST THEM—ONE AT A TIME—OR DO THEY FEEL THAT YOU ARE TOO DISTRACTED BY OTHER CONCERNS?

4. Model Positive Behavior

Your modeling during conversations can set a positive atmosphere that encourages trust and inspires the client to open up to you. We must model behavior that we have observed from those whom we consider to be excellent listeners and role models.

DOES YOUR COMPANY MODEL OTHER COMPANIES WHO YOUR CONSUMERS BELIEVE LISTEN TO THEIR NEEDS?

5. Restatement and Feelings Check

Our goal in becoming an empathetic listener is to listen for content and feeling, understanding the message on all levels. If your intuition tells you that the other person really means something other than what he is saying, check it out. Restate what you believe is the message and combine it with a 'feelings' word to prove or disprove your assumption. For example, when I hear someone say, "I didn't get the service I expected when I called your company," I might reply, "It sounds like you were really disappointed with your last experience." Not only did I restate in other words, what I thought I heard, but I added the word *disappointed*. Now the customer can agree or correct you allowing us to keep on track.

WHEN WAS THE LAST TIME YOU CLARIFIED WHAT YOU THINK YOUR CUSTOMERS ARE SAYING?

6. Ambiguity is Reality

The 500 most commonly used words in English have 14,070 dictionary meanings. It is important that you concentrate on the connotation—what words mean through implication and suggestion—vs. denotation or the specific dictionary meaning.

DOES YOUR MARKET REALLY UNDERSTAND WHAT YOU ARE ATTEMPTING TO ACCOMPLISH?

7. Ask Questions

It seems like such an easy thing to do, but it is probably the most difficult. We are not natural questioners. We naturally want to be the 'giver of information' not the 'seeker'. Change your role and observe the results you get.

ARE YOU ASKING ENOUGH PROBING QUESTIONS OF YOUR CUSTOMERS?

The bottom line is that we can only increase our sales presence by truly listening to our clients. There is a saying I share with all of my training audiences. *Listen to your environment for whispers of opportunity.* Are you really listening for the opportunity in your market?

"Your most valued customers will tell you what can be done with your brand."
Jørgen Vig Knudstorp CEO of LEGO.

Jeff's perspective on listening is vitally important to success as a project manager. This is particularly true if you are trying to take your PM role to a strategically valued position in the enterprise. What you listen to and who you listen to is critical as well. It will demonstrate to your team and to upper management what your true values are, your *north-star* so to speak. If this vision lines up and links from every task your team performs directly to the vision of the organization, then you will find communication will open and success will follow. Listen carefully to the right things.

The quote above by the CEO of LEGO was spoken during a corporate turn-around. In 2003, LEGO was known as a company that did not accept 'unsolicited ideas'. They were also technically bankrupt. Jørgen was brought in as a fresh, young CEO to facilitate the re-calibration. One of the most important things he did, depicted in the book *"Brick by Brick"* by David C. Robertson, was to create direct listening channels from LEGO's customers and partners. The feedback from those new direct interactions at *Brick Fests* (gatherings of LEGO enthusiasts) and other venues gave insight and clarity and direction to Mr. Vig Knudstorp and his team.

Listening, along with the adoption of many Agile practices, caused LEGO to rise from the ashes, returning it to its earlier high performing and profitable history as a leader in the toy industry. From 2007 to 2011 Mattel and Hasbro, the two dominant players in the toy industry, grew at an annual rate of one to three percent LEGO. posted growth of twenty four percent in the same time frame. In 2012 they reported a twenty-seven percent increase in sales and a thirty-six percent increase in profit over the previous year.

Apparently this listening thing worked for LEGO. It will work for you too.

That is The Question

Digging Deeper to Understand your Clients' True Needs

Once again, I have to re-iterate that I believe that everyone is in sales. I have not met a project manager yet who doesn't constantly 'sell' ideas/concepts or change or themselves. There are great lessons to be learned from sales that I think are so relevant to what you do every day.

I recall an incident several years ago, when I had just started my business and one of my sales people, Vic, came to me with exciting news. During his first week "knocking on doors", he had secured a $10,000 order. Now, keep in mind that this was back in 1983 and an order of this magnitude was not a common occurrence.

When I interrogated Vic, I discovered that he only had sketchy details. The client had purchased three thousand imprinted coffee mugs because of a 'supplier special'. I asked Vic, "What are they doing with the mugs?"

He hesitated before answering, "Well, they are going to give them away."

"Who are they giving them to?" I wanted to know.

"I have no idea, but I got the purchase order," Vic answered defensively.

As I pondered this new role, I realized that the transformation from selling stuff to selling solutions, lies in the questions we asked of our clients. As odd as it may seem, I decided that there was a huge difference between a large sale and a small sale. Before you dismiss me as a crackpot, let me explain. It occurred to me, at that moment, that this was a very typical sale in most industries. As long as we get the sale, who cares how the client is using our service or product?

Typically and traditionally, we have defined the size of the sale in terms of dollar amount. What if I told you that I decided that Vic's ten-thousand-dollar sale was actually a 'small' sale? I think we should begin defining the 'large' sale as that *which advances us towards building an on-going relationship with our client*. In other words, the more we position ourselves as a 'counselor' in our business, the more likely we are to develop that long-term relationship that so many of us seek. I guarantee you that Vic had to go in and "sell" that coffee mug client *every time* he visited them. And, selling the client means that you are not taking the time to properly consult with the client and build a long-lasting relationship.

In your new role as counselor, I would encourage you to develop a questionnaire that just includes simple questions that must be answered in order for you to be effective for your client. Although your questions may vary from mine, I have found these very helpful.

• **What are your goals?**

Such a simple question can set us apart as the professionals in our area of expertise. When the client insists that they want one hundred widgets, it is our duty to ask, "Why" or "What do you hope to accomplish with these widgets?" You would be amazed at how many clients have not considered this. They get 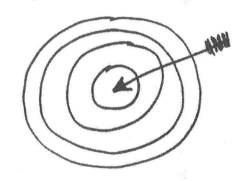 it in their heads that they want sweaters when, in fact, they are going to the equator on their sales trip and golf shirts just may be better received.

• **Who is the target audience?**

There are many times that I find the buyer is purchasing an item or service that they want, not what their recipient wants. Why not sit with the buyer and put together a "recipient profile", a list of characteristics of the end user. You just might surprise the buyer by making them realize

that they need to pay more attention to the demographics
of their audience not their particular likes and dislikes.

• Who makes the buying decision?

So many salespeople forget to ask this going into the sale,
that it sometimes throws the buyer off. One rule in our
office...if this person can't say YES, then who can? If this
person is the person charged with the task of "screening"
vendors, then rehearse them to take the details to the
decision maker. Just make sure you know how the decision
is made and by whom.

• What is the time schedule?

If you have ever participated in any type of goal-setting
course, you were most likely told that goals must be
benchmarked against the acronym, SMART. Every goal
must be Specific, Measurable, Attainable, Realistic and
Timed. This question just zeros in on the 'T'—timed. Then
make sure it fits all of the others and, most important, is
the timing realistic?

• What is the budget and how is it broken down?

I have ulterior motives for asking this question. I want to
know if my sale was part of a larger program or if it was a
stand-alone expenditure. This often helps me in securing

an even larger sale because the client might not realize
that there are other products or services that I can offer as
they relate to this project. Not only that, but I need to have
a workable—and realistic—budget with which to work. I
can't tell you how many times a client suggested a 'range'
of a budget. This doesn't help me in my quest to adhere to
SMART; it is not specific.

• What did you like and dislike about the vendor who supplied you with this product/service last time?

A simple question but an important one if you are to
provide service above and beyond what this person
expects. If you supplied the product last time, ask it about
yourself… you might be surprised by the response.

• Is this project going out for bid?

My favorite question! Be careful if you choose to ask this.
The client will typically come back with, "Why do you want
to know?" Now, I do not promote projecting an image of
your company that you cannot support, but on the other
hand, sometimes you can get around the issue and get
your point across. My reply was always the same…

"If this is going out to bid, I will be happy to give it
to my bid department. If it is *not* going out to bid, I will
give it to my creative department!" Inevitably, the reaction
was the same. Nobody wants to sacrifice creativity when

it comes to their project. More importantly, I refused to spend the same amount of time on a project that was going out for bid.

These are only suggested questions. The important part is that you simply ask more questions. Our roles have changed from the 'giver of information' to that of 'the seeker of information' and the only way that we can do this, is to ask more questions of our clients.

By the way, I am sure you are wondering...we did not refuse the ten-thousand-dollar order for coffee mugs nor did we call the client on the phone and ask "why did you order these?" Hey, we decided to be counselors *after* that sale!

"Successful people ask better questions, and as a result, they get better answers."
Tony Robbins

"Why is project management important? In so many areas of our lives, we use project management without even realizing we are. Whether it's brushing your teeth or building a skyscraper, we all use project management every day. Initiating, planning, executing, monitoring/controlling and closing out every project requires some knowledge and expertise of what you are doing and will be more likely to get completed with a trained project manager. Project managers get things done."

"Hope is not a strategy. Project management provides a framework to help accomplish goals."
From the website of the PMI New York City Chapter.

The Project Management Institute (PMI) in the past few years has been working hard to move project management from being seen as "the people who get things done" to being a strategic partner at the highest level of any organization. They still want technical excellence in project delivery but with a constant focus on the business value that delivery provides. A big hill to climb, no doubt.

One of the key tools in shifting perception from "they make the trains run on time" to "this is our strategic partner" is asking the right questions. Re-craft Jeff's questions for yourself and orient them toward;

- Why are we doing this?
- What is our Vision? Does this project fulfill that vision?
- How are the strategic goals of the organization met by successful completion of this project?
- Etc.

Understand the answers to these questions yourself and then begin to filter every task you and your team act on through this grid. Remember, simplify and continuously narrow what you are doing to the items that will deliver the highest value as defined by the answers to these questions. Create a culture that asks and expects questions but make sure you are asking the right questions.

Now go get things done.

COLORING

The Poem...

Coloring Outside The Lines

Coloring outside the lines is scary business.

Some days, I don't have the courage for it at all.

On my big, bold days though, I like to let my red crayon just streak across the lines

out there with my purple

in perfect freedom—NO LINES!

And coloring outside the lines is lonely too.

I'm the only kid that doesn't get a gold star on my paper.

The teacher frowns. The kids?

They call me weird or dumb or stupid.

Why don't they see?

I'm not behind them. I'm actually out in front—running free—outside the lines.

And, it would be nice to have a friend who colored outside the lines too.

Would you?

Anonymous

Give the Gift of

Coloring Outside the Lines...

To Your Friends and Colleagues

This book is self-published and is easiest ordered right from Jeff Tobe's office!

(tear this page out, fill it in, scan and email it OR mail it to the address at the bottom)

❑ I want to order _____ copies of Coloring Outside the Lines™ at $19.95 each, plus $3 shipping per book (Pennsylvania residents please add $1.20 sales tax per book). Orders for 24 or more books, please call for volume discounts. Canadian orders must be accompanied by a postal money order or check in U.S. funds or call us with credit card information. Allow 10 days for deliver.

❑ My check or money order for $_____ is enclosed.

❑ Please charge my: (circle one) Visa Mastercard Amex

Name: _____

Organization: _____

Address: _____

City/State/Zip:_____

Phone: _____ E-mail: _____

Card Number: _____

Exp. Date:_____ Signature:_____

PLEASE MAKE YOUR CHECK PAYABLE AND RETURN TO:

Coloring Outside the Lines

5311 Friendship Avenue

Call your credit card order to: 1-412-373-6592
E-mail us at: info@JeffTobe.com
Fax: 1-412-373-8773

About the Authors:

Jeff Tobe, M.Ed, CSP

Certified Speaking Professional, Jeff Tobe's credentials are impressive. Insider Magazine dubbed him *"The Guru of Creativity"* and readers of Convention & Meetings Magazine chose him as one of the top 15 speakers in North America. He is a customer experience expert, professional speaker and bestselling author who works with companies and organizations who want to increase their bottom line by changing their customer experience and retaining great talent. He is a popular keynote speaker at diverse forums around the world.

Tobe founded *Coloring Outside the Lines* in 1994 and since then has worked with hundreds of clients ranging from Fortune 500 companies to ones with less than 20 employees including Microsoft, PMI, PNC Bank, Sonny's BBQ and many more!

Jeff Tobe's most requested programs focus on CREATIVITY/ INNOVATION, CUSTOMER EXPERIENCE and EMPLOYEE ENGAGEMENT. His high-energy, high-fun and high-content programs create the ideal presentation for any kind of corporate or educational forum.

His articles have been read in hundreds of publications and he is the author of the hugely popular book, Coloring Outside The Lines. He is the co-author of three other books and his newest book, ANTICIPATE: Knowing What Customers Need Before They Do is quickly becoming one of the hottest business books on the market. Jeff is also the creator of the Touch Point Focus initiative in which he helps clients re-examine their customer touch points

Jeff lives in Pittsburgh, PA with his wife Judy...and YES, he IS a huge Steelers' fan!

Ted Kallman, FCP, FCT, PMP, PMI-ACP, CSM, CSPO, CSP

As an Enterprise Agile Coach, Ted Kallman helps organizations in the common-sense adoption of lean-agile to increase effectiveness and quality, reduce cycle times, and to create a pre-adaptive environment to innovate and create value. Ted is co-author with his brother Andrew of the national best-selling book "The Nehemiah Effect: Ancient Wisdom from the World's First Agile Projects" and "Flow: Beyond Agile" due for release in 2015 and a well-known speaker. Among Ted's many professional designations he is a Certified ScrumMaster (CSM), PMI-Agile Certified Practitioner (PMI-ACP), Project Management Professional (PMP), and one of 2,000 Certified Scrum Professional's in the world. He is a member of the Agile Alliance, founder of Agile West Michigan which is affiliated with the Agile Leadership Network, the Scrum Alliance. He also serves on the Board of the PMI Western Michigan Chapter.

63298523R00133

Made in the USA
Lexington, KY
02 May 2017